TENSE
SITUATIONS

TENSES IN CONTRAST AND CONTEXT

PAMELA HARTMANN • PATRICIA ESPARZA
ANNETTE ZARIAN

Harcourt Brace & Company

Orlando   San Diego   New York
Toronto   London   Sydney   Tokyo

ACKNOWLEDGMENTS

The authors would like to thank Jean Zukowski/Faust and Anne Boynton-Trigg of Holt, Rinehart and Winston; Yves Jacot for the initial inspiration; our patient reviewers (Lida Baker, of UCLA; Gloria Brambilla, of the Los Angeles Unified School District; and Judy Gough, of Santa Monica College); Ann Snow of UCLA, for help with the appendix; Don Robb, for uncomplainingly squeezing casts of thousands into incredibly small spaces; Elaine Kirn, without whose foresight and persistence this book would never have found its way to a publisher and without whose editing skills it wouldn't be what it is; and all ESL students and teachers who have used, are using, and will be using this book.

LIBRARY OF CONGRESS CATALOGING IN PUBLICATION DATA

Main entry under title:

TENSE SITUATIONS: Tenses in Contrast and Context
Includes appendix

1. English Language Textbook for foreigners. I. Pamela Hartmann, Annette A. Zarian, Patricia S. Esparza
84-48116

ISBN 0-03-069902-9

Address Editorial Correspondence to:
6277 Sea Harbor Drive
Orlando, Florida 32887

Printed in the United States of America

3 4 066 12 11 10

TEACHER'S NOTES

TENSE SITUATIONS is intended for high-intermediate ESL students who have studied all or most of the tenses in English but haven't mastered them completely. Such students may have difficulty "juggling" several tenses at once because they have studied each tense in isolation or, at best, in contrast with only one other tense. In addition, they may not have studied any tense within a complete context. It's important for students at this stage to learn to integrate the various tenses and to understand the shades of meaning of each tense; TENSE SITUATIONS guides students toward this end by focusing on tenses *in contrast* and *in the context* of complete stories. Frequent review and recycling prevents students from forgetting one tense as they learn a new one.

This text can be useful as either a self-study book or a classroom textbook for students who know about the various tenses but don't use them in free conversation or writing. Instead, these students tend to fixate on just a few select tenses: the simple present ("I write a letter right now."), simple past ("I drove down the freeway when I saw an accident."), and simple future with "will" ("I will watch TV tonight."). Their use of the language is stilted, unnatural, and often ungrammatical because of their inability to utilize the complete range of tenses.

TENSE SITUATIONS can also be used as a reference by teachers and students alike. Rules for the use of each tense are found within the chapters; in addition, the appendix offers a series of charts on (1) the use of non-action verbs, and (2) the use of tenses in subordinate clauses, indirect speech, the passive voice, and the basic conditional.

The book was not intended to encompass all facets of verb usage. Modals, the conditional, the passive voice, and indirect speech have not been included, except in the appendix, so that attention may be focused on a thorough treatment of the tenses themselves. One chapter, for example, is devoted to the difference between "will" and "be going to"; this difference is often ignored in ESL classrooms but needs to be mastered if the student is to avoid awkward, unnatural, or misleading language.

The art work used throughout the text is, for the most part, functional. An attempt has been made to portray the abstract notions of time and tense as concretely—as visually—as possible. The careful arrangement of pictures within the frames in the filmstrip stories allows students to visualize the relationship of one tense to another; wherever possible, "before now" or "before then" is to the left, and "after now" or "after then" is to the right, corresponding to the notion of the time lines on which "past" is to the left and "future" is to the right. For example, in the filmstrip story depicting future perfect, the narrator ("now") is placed in the far left corner of the frame and the "future" action on the far right. The "future perfect" action is placed in a bubble to the left of the "future," signifying its placement in time—that is, before another future action.

The authors hope that the use of humorous—sometimes outrageous—characters and situations will make this sometimes insufferable subject not only sufferable but, perhaps, even enjoyable!

USE OF THE BOOK

All chapters except for the review chapters should be presented using the following steps:

1. Students read the filmstrip story on the left of the page. The teacher may introduce new vocabulary before students begin to read the filmstrip story or may check their understanding of it afterwards. Most new vocabulary items have been recycled elsewhere in the text.
2. Students then go back to the beginning, cover up the story on the left, and read the story on the right; this time they choose the correct tense for each simple verb form.
3. Students read the explanations. (Depending on the students' level, steps 1 and 2 may be done in reverse order.) Whenever possible, the explanations contain examples taken from the filmstrip stories. Because space limitations have restricted the number of examples that could be included, teachers may want to point out additional examples from the filmstrip story or from their students' lives.
4. The teacher guides students through the DIRECTIONS and EXAMPLES for the Rap It Up section (oral exercises). Then students work in pairs independently of the teacher.

5. For the Fill It In section or the Picture Puzzle (alternate chapters), the teacher guides students through the first few sentences. The Picture Puzzles will probably require additional explanation, at least initially. One successful method is for the teacher to put many of the picture puzzle symbols and one sample sentence on the blackboard, silently point to each, and have the class guess the meanings before actually beginning to write. The students soon learn the common symbols and have little need for the Key to Symbols at the back of the book.

For the review chapters:

1. Students fill in the blanks in the story.
2. Students rewrite the story—without looking back at it—with the aid of the Cue Sheet.
3. Using the information on the Story Line, students answer the questions on the next page. This may be done orally or in writing, depending on the level and focus of the class.
4. Students practice the targeted tenses in role play or discussion related to their own lives.

For the cumulative review chapters:

1. Students fill in the blanks in the story. Because these stories are quite long, they have been divided into sections. Students might do section 1 in class, section 2 for homework, and section 3 in class the next day. The teacher should encourage the class to keep in mind the entire context instead of concentrating on each sentence as a separate entity.
2. Students work in pairs or groups on the Rap It Up section.

ANSWER KEYS:

For the sake of style and the use of natural language, contractions have been used wherever possible. Where several tenses are possible in a given situation, these have been indicated. The teacher may refer students to explanation pages or reference charts if there is any confusion. It may sometimes be frustrating to find multiple possibilities; however, this is the nature of the language, and to present exercises without such complexity would mean creating unnatural linguistic situations.

CONTENTS

PRESENT

PRESENT CONTINUOUS
SIMPLE PRESENT

DIRECTIONS: Read the story on the left. When you finish, go back to the beginning, cover up the story to the left, and choose the correct tense for each capitalized simple form of the verb to the right of the picture.

My name is James Sterling. I'm the cruise director on the "Holiday Princess." Every week our ship *sails* around the Caribbean full of passengers.

My name is James Sterling. I'm the cruise director on the "Holiday Princess." Every week our ship SAIL around the Caribbean full of passengers.

The people on the ship *are* always *looking* for fun and excitement. Let's look at some of the people on board this week.

The people on the ship always LOOK for fun and excitement. Let's look at some of the people on board this week.

Here *is* Mr. Rodney Tyler. He *is* a very charming man. He *is enjoying* this trip very much right now.

Here BE Mr. Rodney Tyler. He BE a very charming man. He ENJOY this trip very much right now.

At this moment he *is sitting* in the middle of a group of women.

At this moment he SIT in the middle of a group of women.

He *is entertaining* them with funny stories, *offering* them champagne, and *laughing* at their jokes.

In his everyday life, however, Rodney Tyler *is* a very shy man.

He *is working* temporarily as a librarian. At work, he *sits* by himself among the books in the library.

He rarely *looks* at people and usually *spends* his time daydreaming.

And there *is* Mr. Horace Pennington III. He *is relaxing* this week.

Look! He *is lying* in his chair and *reading* a novel. And *isn't* there music coming from the radio beside him?

He ENTERTAIN them with funny stories, OFFER them champagne, and LAUGH at their jokes.

In his everyday life, however, Rodney Tyler BE a very shy man.

He WORK temporarily as a librarian. At work, he SIT by himself among the books in the library.

He rarely LOOK at people and usually SPEND his time daydreaming.

And there BE Mr. Horace Pennington III. He RELAX this week.

Look! He LIE in his chair and READ a novel. And NOT BE there music coming from the radio beside him?

At home, by contrast, Horace Pennington never *relaxes*.

He hardly ever *reads* novels; instead, every morning he *reads* the business news in the "Wall Street Journal". . .

. . . and *listens* to the news of the stock market on his car radio as he *goes* to work.

Why, I *don't believe* my eyes. *Is* that Ellen Wiggley?

Look, she's *jogging* around the ship!

My gosh, now she's even *doing* jumping jacks!

At home, by contrast, Horace Pennington never RELAX.

He hardly ever READ novels; instead, every morning he READ the business news in the "Wall Street Journal". . .

. . . and LISTEN to the news of the stock market on his car radio as he GO to work.

Why, I NOT BELIEVE my eyes. BE that Ellen Wiggley?

Look, she JOG around the ship!

My gosh, now she even DO jumping jacks!

This is amazing! When Ellen is at home, she's always *complaining* and *saying* that she *wants* to jog and exercise, but somehow she rarely *does* more than watch TV.

Now the ship *is coming* back to port. The passengers *are thinking* about changing their everyday lives. Rodney *hopes* to always enjoy life as he *is enjoying* it at this moment.

Horace *is promising* himself to relax as he *is relaxing* at present.

And Ellen *wants* to exercise as she *is doing* right now.

Ah. Here they all are now. They*'re leaving* the ship.

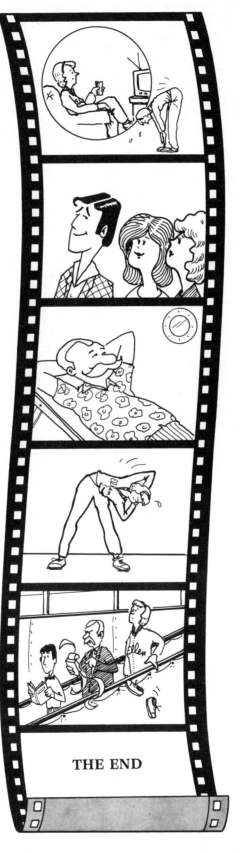

THE END

This is amazing! When Ellen is at home, she always COMPLAIN and SAY that she WANT to jog and exercise, but somehow she rarely DO more than watch TV.

Now the ship COME back to port. The passengers THINK about changing their everyday lives. Rodney HOPE to always enjoy life as he ENJOY it at this moment.

Horace PROMISE himself to relax as he RELAX at present.

And Ellen WANT to exercise as she DO right now.

Ah. Here they all are now. They LEAVE the ship.

PRESENT CONTINUOUS	SIMPLE PRESENT

1. The PRESENT CONTINUOUS expresses an action that is happening right now.

———————————|———————————
                              NOW

They're *leaving* the ship.

NON-ACTION verbs do not usually occur in the PRESENT CONTINUOUS. (See the Appendix, page 155-157.)

The SIMPLE PRESENT is used with a NON-ACTION verb to indicate something that is happening right now.

———————————|———————————
                              NOW

She *seems* happy.
This *tastes* good.
I *don't believe* my eyes!

See the Appendix for a list of these verbs.

2. The PRESENT CONTINUOUS also expresses an action (repeated or of long duration) in a time period that *includes* the present moment. However, the action is not necessarily happening right now. The PRESENT CONTINUOUS is used in this way for a *temporary* activity.

                              NOW

Rodney Tyler *is working* temporarily as a librarian.

                              NOW

Horace Pennington *is relaxing* this week.

The SIMPLE PRESENT expresses:
a. an action that is repeated habitually (for example: often, sometimes, every day, once a week);

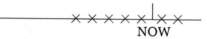
                              NOW

He *reads* the business news every morning.

b. a general truth that is repeated periodically;

The sun *sets* in the west.

c. a condition that is not repeated but is always true.

———————————|———————————
                              NOW

Ellen Wiggley *loves* chocolate.

3. The PRESENT CONTINUOUS is used for a very frequent activity about which we feel some emotion. We use it with the adverbs *always, forever,* or *constantly.*

                              NOW

She's always *complaining.* (irritation)

The adverb comes between *BE* and the present participle.

4.		In casual conversation, especially in lengthy narration, the SIMPLE PRESENT can refer to past events. ''So she *runs* into the room and *screams* that there's a UFO on the lawn.''
5.	We often use the PRESENT CONTINUOUS after the word *while*. *While* indicates a continuous action at the same time as another action. There are two possible positions in the sentence for a clause beginning with *while*. While his brothers *are helping* the passengers on the boat, Mark just sits there and does nothing. (comma) Mark just sits there and does nothing while his brothers *are helping* the passengers. (no comma)	When the SIMPLE PRESENT is used after *while*, it indicates a continuous action. She *tries* to look like a normal shopper while she *does* her job catching shoplifters. (For more on *while*, see Chapters 6 and 15.)
6.	When we have a compound verb, the verb BE is omitted from the second action. He *is lying* in his deck chair and *reading* a novel.	

7.	We often use the PRESENT CONTINUOUS with these words:
	
	see box #1 (right) now
	             at the (this) moment
	             at present
	
	see box #2 these days, nowadays
	             today
	             this week, month, year
	             this semester, quarter, and so on
	
	see box #3 always
	             forever
	             constantly
		We often use the SIMPLE PRESENT with these words:
		
		always
		often
		frequently
		usually
		sometimes
		every day, week, month, and so on
		once a week, month, year, and so on
		occasionally
		seldom
		rarely
		never

For additional uses of the PRESENT CONTINUOUS and SIMPLE PRESENT, see Chapters 14 and 15.

DIRECTIONS: **A.** Work with one other student. Make up as many sentences as you can about the following pictures. Use the PRESENT CONTINUOUS and SIMPLE PRESENT tenses. Use the vocabulary at the bottom of the page to help you describe the pictures.

The Nile Queen is now sailing down the Nile River. Here are three passengers. What are they doing now, and what do they usually do at home?

Examples: She is playing shuffleboard (now/at this moment/and so on).
She (usually/often/sometimes/and so on) sits in a rocking chair.

On the cruise
At home

Grandmother

Policeman

Actress

VOCABULARY			
shuffleboard	pyramids	to knit	to climb
rocking chair	camel	to arrest	to put on makeup
robbers	crowd	to rescue	to sign
hippopotamus	autograph book	to drown	

B. Have a TELEPHONE CONVERSATION. Find a partner in class. Pretend you and your family are on a trip right now. Describe to your partner what you and your family are doing on the trip. Use the time expressions and verb phrases from the left columns in the boxes below as well as your own ideas. Your partner will answer you by telling you what he/she does every day, using words from the right columns in the boxes below and his/her own ideas.

Example: —Hello, Tom, I'm calling from Paris. We're having a wonderful time this week.
         We're doing a lot of sightseeing.
         —Hi, Mary, everything here is the same. I do the same things every day.
         I get up. . .

TIME EXPRESSIONS	
right now	every day
at this moment	usually
on this trip	often
today	always
this week	on Mondays
	every Wednesday

VERB PHRASES	
take a train, bus, boat, and so on	get up
take pictures	have breakfast, lunch, dinner
take a tour	go to school
go sightseeing	do the dishes
buy souvenirs	go shopping
set up a tent	play tennis
go hiking	read
go swimming	watch TV
go fishing	do homework
	go to bed

C. Exchange roles and repeat the above exercise.

DIRECTIONS: Fill in the blanks in the following story with the SIMPLE PRESENT or PRESENT CONTINUOUS tense. A check mark (✔) indicates that more than one tense may be possible in some of the blanks.

THE FISHING TRIP

Gordon and his three sons, Mark, Joe, and Leo, (1)_____(own) a charter fishing boat. Every day when they (2)_____ (sail), they (3)_____ (take) a boat full of would-be fishermen out to sea. Leo, the youngest, (4)_____ (sell) tickets every afternoon for the next day's trip. The passengers (5)_____ (arrive) now with high hopes. Some (6)_____ (carry) their own equipment, and others (7)_____ (rent) it from Gordon.

Usually when everyone (8)_____ (be) aboard, Gordon (9)_____ (stand) at the wheel and (10)_____ (signal) Mark to untie the boat. But today Mark (11)_____ (daydream), so Joe (12)_____ (loosen) the rope and (13)_____ (throw) it on the boat. Gordon always (14)_____ (start) the motor while Joe (15)_____✔ (prepare) the bait. On the way out, Leo sometimes (16)_____ (give) the fishermen ideas on how to fish. When Gordon (17)_____ (find) a good spot, Leo (18)_____ (drop) anchor and the fishermen (19)_____ (throw) out their lines.

Today, they (20)_____ (fish) in one of Gordon's favorite spots. Gordon (21)_____ (tell) his favorite fish stories. Some of the passengers (22)_____ (eat) their lunch, while others, who (23)_____✔ (not feel) well, (24)_____ (try) not to look at the food or smell the bait. One of the fishermen (25)_____ (reel) in a fish. His friend (26)_____ (take) his picture.

Leo and Joe (27)_____ (help) some of the passengers bait their hooks. Mark (28)_____ (also try) to help. Poor Mark! He (29)_____✔ (always try) to be useful, but usually (30)_____ (end up) causing some damage. He (31)_____ (forever trip) over ropes, (32)_____ (fall) over the anchor, or (33)_____ (get) tangled in the fishermen's lines. At this moment, while his brothers (34)_____✔ (help) the passengers, Mark (35)_____ (lean) out of the boat to catch one of the fishermen's stubborn fish with his net. The fish (36)_____ (jump) in all directions. Oh, oh, it (37)_____ (seem) that the fish (38)_____ (win). Mark (39)_____ (fall) overboard. He never (40)_____(know) when to give up.

2 PRESENT PERFECT
SIMPLE PRESENT

DIRECTIONS: Read the story on the left. When you finish, go back to the beginning, cover up the story to the left, and choose the correct tense for each capitalized simple form of the verb to the right of the picture.

ELMER KADIDDLE

It's Elmer Kadiddle's 100th birthday today.

It BE Elmer Kadiddle's 100th birthday today.

Elmer *has* never *been* sick a day in his life. He *has* never *taken* any medicine or *been* to any doctors.

Elmer NEVER BE sick a day in his life. He NEVER TAKE any medicine or BE to any doctors.

Elmer *lives* on a farm in Nebraska.

Elmer LIVE on a farm in Nebraska.

He's *lived* on the same farm since he was born.

He LIVE on the same farm since he was born.

Elmer *has gotten up* at sunrise every day of his life. He*'s fed* the chickens and *gathered* the eggs since he was old enough to walk.

Elmer GET UP at sunrise every day of his life. He FEED the chickens and GATHER the eggs since he was old enough to walk.

He*'s milked* the cows without missing a day— even his wedding day.

He MILK the cows without missing a day— even his wedding day.

Elmer *has been* married to the same woman for the last 80 years.

Elmer BE married to the same woman for the last 80 years.

His wife, Iona, *grows* all their vegetables in her garden.

His wife, Iona, GROW all their vegetables in her garden.

She *cans* fruits and vegetables, and every day she *bakes* her own bread.

She CAN fruits and vegetables, and every day she BAKE her own bread.

Iona and Elmer *have been* happily married since their wedding day. Their only arguments *have been* about their son, Elmer, Jr.

Iona and Elmer BE happily married since their wedding day. Their only arguments BE about their son, Elmer, Jr.

Junior *is* nothing like his father. He *hates* farm life.

Junior BE nothing like his father. He HATE farm life.

Elmer *complains* that Junior *has* never *done* a day's work in his life.

Elmer COMPLAIN that Junior NEVER DO a day's work in his life.

Junior usually *gets up* at noon, and his mother always *has* a big breakfast waiting for him.

Junior usually GET UP at noon, and his mother always HAVE a big breakfast waiting for him.

After breakfast, he often *goes* fishing.

After breakfast, he often GO fishing.

But he *doesn't catch* very many fish.

But he NOT CATCH very many fish.

Junior *spends* Saturday nights playing the guitar for his friends.

Junior SPEND Saturday nights playing the guitar for his friends.

He *has dreamed* about going to the big city since he was a young boy.

But, as Elmer *says*, there *is* no need to worry; Junior *is* too lazy to pack.

Elmer and Iona *have argued* about this again and again for years.

Elmer *says* it's time for the boy to settle down and get to work.

Iona *says* to give him time; he's just a boy. After all, he's barely 59 years old.

THE END

He DREAM about going to the big city since he was a young boy.

But, as Elmer SAY, there BE no need to worry; Junior BE too lazy to pack.

Elmer and Iona ARGUE about this again and again for years.

Elmer SAY it BE time for the boy to settle down and get to work.

Iona SAY to give him time; he BE just a boy. After all, he BE barely 59 years old.

PRESENT PERFECT	SIMPLE PRESENT

1.

One use of the PRESENT PERFECT is to express an activity happening *now*. Something in the sentence or context tells us when the action began. The action may be continuous or periodic.

Elmer and Iona *have been* happily married since their wedding day 80 years ago. (continuously)

He *has milked* the cows all his life without missing a day. (periodic)

The PRESENT PERFECT may be used with both ACTION and NON-ACTION verbs.

With the SIMPLE PRESENT, there is no indication of when the action began or how long it has gone on.

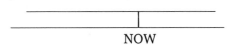

Elmer and Iona *are* happily married.

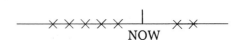

He *milks* the cows every morning.

2.

We often use the PRESENT PERFECT with the words *for* or *since*. *For* tells us the length of the action, and *since* indicates the point in time when the action began. Here are some examples of time expressions.

for	since
5 minutes	6:00
2 weeks	April 23
3 years	1980
several days	the accident
a long time	I was young
*the past week	last week

Elmer *has been* married to the same woman for 80 years.

He *has lived* on the same farm since he was born.

We don't use the SIMPLE PRESENT with *since*.

*NOTE: The PAST TENSE (Chapter 5) is used with *last* (week, month, year, and so on). But <u>the past (last)</u> week, month, and so on usually includes "now," so it is often used with the PRESENT PERFECT.

Iona *was* sick *last week*.
Iona *has been* sick for *the last week*.

We also use the PRESENT PERFECT with expressions such as:

all day (week, year, and so on)
so far
up until now
all (his/her/my/and so on) life

Junior *has hated* the farm all his life.

3. When we have a compound verb, the verb HAVE is omitted from the second action.

He*'s fed* the chickens and *gathered* eggs since he was old enough to walk.

For other uses of the PRESENT PERFECT, see Chapter 5.

RAP IT UP

DIRECTIONS: A. Work with a partner. For each picture on the next page, make up two logical sentences. In the first tell what people do every day. In the second tell *for how long* or *since when* they have done these things. Use the time expressions in the column at the right in the second sentence. Make as many sentences as you can.

Example: Elmer is a farmer.
He's been a farmer for a long time.

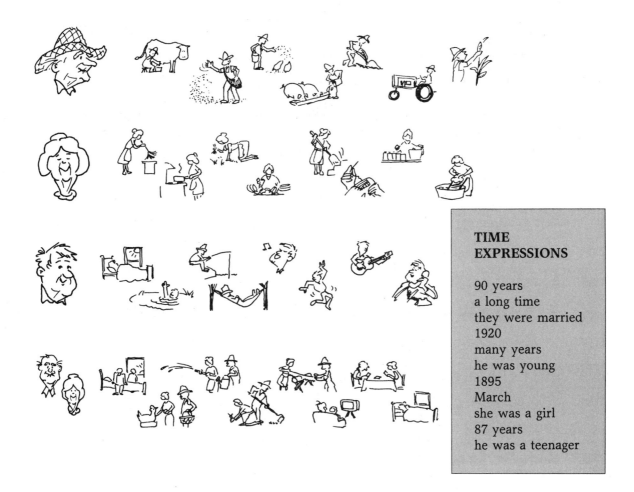

**TIME
EXPRESSIONS**

90 years
a long time
they were married
1920
many years
he was young
1895
March
she was a girl
87 years
he was a teenager

B. Tell your partner about your life. Use as many of the following verbs as possible as well as verbs of your own. Use the SIMPLE PRESENT and the PRESENT PERFECT tenses.

Example: I get up at 7:00 every day. I've gotten up at 7:00 every day for many years. I've never gone sailing.

VERB PHRASES

get up (when?)	owe money to. . .	want. . .
live (where?)	own a car, bicycle,	need a new car, shirt,
work (where?)	and so on	and so on
study (what?)	belong to me	like. . .
clean the house	go sailing	have. . .
play soccer	go fishing	be a student
know how to. . .	believe	be happy
	understand English	be a secretary

DIRECTIONS: On another piece of paper, write out the following story. Change all of the pictures and symbols to words. The character's name (🏃) is Norbert (Elmer's brother), but you should use pronouns (*he, him*) whenever possible. For each of the encircled verbs, choose the SIMPLE PRESENT or the PRESENT PERFECT. In a few cases, more than one tense may be possible. If you can't guess the meaning of a symbol, check page 163 in the Appendix.

NORBERT'S LIFE

ELMER'S BROTHER, 🏃, (BE) 97 & (LIVE) ALONE ⊠ THE [city]. 🏃 (LIVE) THERE SINCE 🏃 LEFT THE [farm] 75 YEARS AGO. 🏃 (HAVE) AN APARTMENT ⌂ THE TOP FLOOR OF A [building] FOR THE PAST 20 YEARS.

🏃 (BE) A VERY CHARMING PERSON, SO 🏃 (HAVE) A LOT OF FRIENDS & (LEAD) A BUSY LIFE. 🏃 ALMOST NEVER (GET) [out] OF [bed] BEFORE [clock] EACH [sunrise] BECAUSE 🏃 USUALLY (STAY) ↑ LATE AT [moon]. 🏃 (LIKE) → PLAY [cards] W/ HIS FRIENDS ⊠ THE AFTER [clock]. SOMETIMES 🏃 (GO) → THE [horse] RACES, & 🏃 ALWAYS (WIN) A LOT OF [money]. ⊠ THE (P.M.) 🏃 USUALLY (TAKE) HIS [woman] → AN $↑ RESTAURANT. 🏃 (KNOW) [woman] FOR ⊠ 30 YEARS, BUT 🏃 (FEEL) THAT 🏃 (BE) READY → GET MARRIED.

🏃 (KNOW) THAT MANY [people] (SPEND) EVERY AFTER [clock] ⊠ THE [park], WHERE THEY (SIT) ⌂ A [bench] & (FEED) THE [bird]s. BUT 🏃 (NEVER GO) ⊠→ THE [park] SINCE 🏃 CAME → THE [city] BECAUSE 🏃 (THINK) THAT ONLY ELDERLY [people] (GO) → [park]s.

EVERY SUMMER, 🏃 (TAKE) A [train] ↓ → HIS BROTHER'S [farm] & (SPEND) SOME TIME THERE. 🏃 (BE) THERE RIGHT NOW. 🏃 (ONLY BE) THERE FOR 5 [sunrise]s, BUT 🏃 (BE) READY → GO BACK → THE [city].

🏃 & HIS BROTHER ELMER (BE) VERY DIFFERENT FROM EACH OTHER, & THEY (ARGUE) ABOUT EVERYTHING EVER SINCE 🏃 ARRIVED ⌂ TUESDAY. THE PROBLEM (BE) THAT 🏃 (NEVER LIKE) THE LIFE OF A FARMER. 🏃 (COMPLAIN) FOR 4 DAYS ABOUT GETTING ↑ AT [sunrise] ↑ & HELPING ELMER W/ THE [cow]s. 🏃 (FEED) THE [chicken]s & (GATHER) 08 ALL WEEK, BUT 🏃 (ENJOY) IT. THE TRUTH (BE) THAT 🏃 (HATE) ANIMALS. 🏃 (THINK) THAT [horse]s (BELONG) ⊠ THE RACES & [sheep]s (BELONG) ⊠ THE [sheep], & 🏃 (BE) SURE THAT [people] (BELONG) ⊠ A [city]!

ELMER'S WIFE, IONA, (BE) WORRIED ABOUT [☺]'S HEALTH FOR MANY YEARS. SHE (FEED) [☺] HOMEMADE SOUP & FRESH [bread] ALL WEEK, & SHE (MAKE) [☺] GO → [bed] AT 9:00 EVERY [moon]. [☺]'S WORST PROBLEM (BE) THAT SHE (TRY) SINCE TUESDAY → PERSUADE [☺] → SETTLE ↓ & GET MARRIED → HIS [woman]. [☺] (HEAR) THIS FROM HER FOR MANY YEARS. EVERY TIME, [☺] (SIGH) & (TELL) HER THE SAME THING: THAT [☺] (BE) A BACHELOR ALL HIS LIFE, & [☺] (W̶A̶N̶T̶) → CHANGE NOW.

PRESENT PERFECT CONTINUOUS
PRESENT CONTINUOUS

DIRECTIONS: Read the story on the left. When you finish, go back to the beginning, cover up the story to the left, and choose the correct tense for each capitalized simple form of the verb to the right of the picture.

—Hey, Joey, what *are* you *doing*?

—Hey, Joey, what you DO?

—I'*m getting* ready to say good-bye to this place.

—I GET ready to say good-bye to this place.

—Ha, that's a good one! You know you have another 15 years to spend in here.

—Ha, that's a good one! You know you have another 15 years to spend in here.

—Yeah, but I'*ve been thinking* that on the outside, those could be the best 15 years of my life. So I'*m getting* out of here now.

—Yeah, but I THINK that on the outside, those could be the best 15 years of my life. So I GET out of here now.

—For the last three months, Shorty, I*'ve been digging* a tunnel.

—No kidding! Where *have* you *been digging* this tunnel?

—It starts under the bunk in my cell and goes out beyond the main gate.

—For the last few days I*'ve been trying* to finish the last part of the tunnel, but I*'m having* a lot of trouble.

—What's the trouble, Joey?

—It*'s been going* too slowly since Lefty stopped helping. I need a strong partner to help me.

—For the last three months, Shorty, I DIG a tunnel.

—No kidding! Where you DIG this tunnel?

—It starts under the bunk in my cell and goes out beyond the main gate.

—For the last few days I TRY to finish the last part of the tunnel, but I HAVE a lot of trouble.

—What's the trouble, Joey?

—It GO too slowly since Lefty stopped helping. I need a strong partner to help me.

—No problem, Joey. I am strong. By the way, what *have* you *been doing* with the dirt, anyway?

—Well, Shorty, you know you*'ve been complaining* the last few months about the food tasting strange. Well, there's a reason for that.

—Oh, no, Joey, not that!
—Too late to worry about it now, pal! Come on. Let's get in the tunnel.

—Even on the eggs, Joey? Is that why the eggs *have been tasting* funny?

—Hurry up! The guards *are coming.*

—We*'ve been crawling* for an awfully long time, Joey. Are you sure we*'re going* in the right direction?

—No problem, Joey. I am strong. By the way, what you DO with the dirt, anyway?

—Well, Shorty, you know you COMPLAIN the last few months about the food tasting strange. Well, there's a reason for that.

—Oh, no, Joey, not that!
—Too late to worry about it now, pal! Come on. Let's get in the tunnel.

—Even on the eggs, Joey? Is that why the eggs TASTE funny?

—Hurry up! The guards COME.

—We CRAWL for an awfully long time, Joey. Are you sure we GO in the right direction?

—I'm positive. *I've been using* this map that Lefty gave me before he left.

—This is it. This is what*'s been giving* me trouble for the past week.

—No problem, Joey, give me a hand.

—Come on, Shorty. We*'re getting* closer.

—Well, hello, boys. *I've been waiting* for you to show up.

THE END

—I'm positive. I USE this map that Lefty gave me before he left.

—This is it. This is what GIVE me trouble for the past week.

—No problem, Joey, give me a hand.

—Come on, Shorty. We GET closer.

—Well, hello, boys. I WAIT for you to show up.

1.

The PRESENT PERFECT CONTINUOUS, like the PRESENT PERFECT, expresses an action that began in the past and is continuing *now*. The action may be continuous or periodic.

She's *been waiting* since 2:00. (continuously)

For the last three months, I've *been digging* a tunnel. (periodically; a little bit each day)

Sometimes the indication of when the action began is not in the sentence. It's only in the mind of the speaker.

I've *been waiting* for you to show up.

The PRESENT CONTINUOUS also expresses an action happening *now*, but there is no indication of when it began.

|
NOW

She's *waiting* over there.

2.

EXCEPTION: We often use the PRESENT PERFECT CONTINUOUS for a finished action if:

a. the action ended very close to "now" *and;*
b. we want to emphasize long duration or hardship.

Oh, there you are! I've *been looking* for you everywhere!

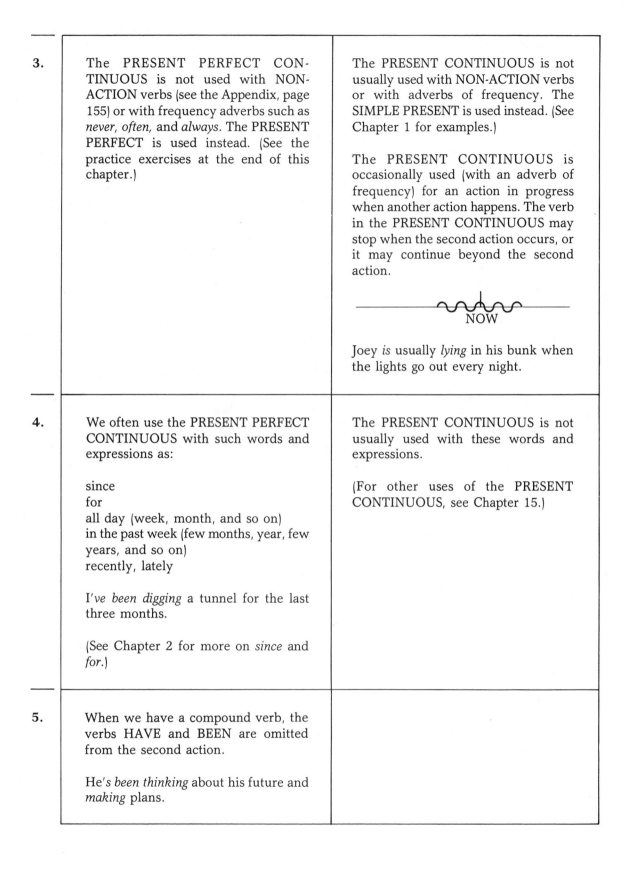

3.	The PRESENT PERFECT CONTINUOUS is not used with NON-ACTION verbs (see the Appendix, page 155) or with frequency adverbs such as *never, often,* and *always.* The PRESENT PERFECT is used instead. (See the practice exercises at the end of this chapter.)	The PRESENT CONTINUOUS is not usually used with NON-ACTION verbs or with adverbs of frequency. The SIMPLE PRESENT is used instead. (See Chapter 1 for examples.) The PRESENT CONTINUOUS is occasionally used (with an adverb of frequency) for an action in progress when another action happens. The verb in the PRESENT CONTINUOUS may stop when the second action occurs, or it may continue beyond the second action. NOW Joey *is* usually *lying* in his bunk when the lights go out every night.
4.	We often use the PRESENT PERFECT CONTINUOUS with such words and expressions as: since for all day (week, month, and so on) in the past week (few months, year, few years, and so on) recently, lately I'*ve been digging* a tunnel for the last three months. (See Chapter 2 for more on *since* and *for.*)	The PRESENT CONTINUOUS is not usually used with these words and expressions. (For other uses of the PRESENT CONTINUOUS, see Chapter 15.)
5.	When we have a compound verb, the verbs HAVE and BEEN are omitted from the second action. He'*s been thinking* about his future and *making* plans.	

DIRECTIONS: **A.** Work with a partner. Look at the picture below and take turns asking and answering questions about what the people are doing.

Example: —What is the man in cell #6 doing?
              —He's sawing the bars on the window.

B. Now go back to the picture above. Ask and answer questions about *how long* the people in the picture have been doing what they are doing.

Example: —How long has the man in cell #6 been sawing?
              —He's been sawing since this morning.

C. Work with a partner. Take the roles of the people in one of the pairs below. You have not seen each other for a long time. Make up a conversation. Use the PRESENT CONTINUOUS and PRESENT PERFECT CONTINUOUS tenses.

two neighbors	doctor and patient
two friends	ex-husband and wife

Example: —Hi, Susan, how are you? What have you been doing?
              —Hello, Jerry, I'm fine. I've been. . . And you?
              —I've been. . .

DIRECTIONS: Fill in the blanks in the following story with the PRESENT PERFECT CONTINUOUS or the PRESENT CONTINUOUS tense. Remember a check mark (✔) indicates that more than one tense may be possible in some of the blanks.

Joey and Shorty are still in prison. One of the prison guards is now making his monthly report on the prisoners to the warden.

PROGRESS REPORT ON JOEY AND SHORTY

—Guard, how are the two prisoners, Joey and Shorty, doing?

—Well, Warden, Shorty (1)_____ (do) very well lately. He is practically a model prisoner. He (2)_____ ✔ (work) very hard. He (3)_____ (always volunteer) for the jobs that no one wants to do. He (4)_____ (constantly sweep) the floors and (5)_____ (clean) the cells. For months he (6)_____ (do) some of Joey's jobs. For the past week, he (7)_____ (work) in the prison kitchen in place of Joey; he (8)_____ (peel) potatoes, (9)_____ (chop) onions, and (10)_____ (wash) the dishes.

—That's excellent, guard, but what about Joey? How (11)_____ ✔ (Joey do)?

—Joey is not exactly a model prisoner. At the moment he (12)_____ (work) on three different plans that we know of to escape from prison. For months now he (13)_____ (try) to build a ladder with anything he can. His friends (14)_____ ✔ (bring) him pieces of sticks, blankets, and even socks. Joey (15)_____ ✔ (use) these to make a ladder. The poor guy (16)_____ ✔ (stay up) nights to make his unusual ladder. What he doesn't know is that we (17)_____ ✔ (only wait) for him to finish before we take it away from him.

Something else that he. . . why, look, warden, what is that commotion over there? That guard (18)_____ (look) inside a garbage can. I think he (19)_____ (talk) to someone. Look, he (20)_____ (pull) Joey out of the garbage can. I'm sure Joey (21)_____ ✔ (try) to escape again. He (22)_____ (try) to get thrown out with the garbage since February. He (23)_____ (always look) for a way to get out. For years now he (24)_____ (bribe) the guards, (25)_____ (steal) keys, and (26)_____ (saw) the bars to try to escape.

—Thank you, guard. I'm going to write all of this in a letter to the judge. Maybe Joey's going to stay with us longer than he thinks.

PRESENT PERFECT CONTINUOUS	PRESENT PERFECT
1. The PRESENT PERFECT CONTINUOUS is not usually used with NON-ACTION verbs (see Appendix, page 155) or with frequency adverbs such as *never, often,* and *always.* He's *been dreaming* for a long time of getting out.	The PRESENT PERFECT is used with NON-ACTION verbs and with frequency adverbs such as *never, often,* and *always.* He's often *dreamed* of getting out.
2. The PRESENT PERFECT CONTINUOUS is not used with a specific amount or a specific number of times. For example, we do not use the PRESENT PERFECT CONTINUOUS with such phrases as *two times, 55 pounds,* or *$135.00.* He's *been trying* to escape all month.	With a specific amount or a specific number of times, we use the PRESENT PERFECT instead of the PRESENT PERFECT CONTINUOUS. He's *tried* to escape twice.

FILL IT IN

DIRECTIONS: Fill in the blanks with the PRESENT PERFECT or the PRESENT PERFECT CONTINUOUS tense. Both tenses are possible with ACTION verbs, but the PRESENT PERFECT CONTINUOUS is more commonly used.

1. Joey and Shorty _____ (do) a lot of digging in the past month.

2. The guards _____ (often see) Joey trying to escape.

3. Shorty _____ (be) a model prisoner for two months.

4. He _____ (mop) the floors since this morning.

5. Joey _____ (study) maps of the prison for the past year.

6. Joey and Shorty _____ (know) each other for three years.

7. Joey _____ (owe) Shorty money for two years.

8. Joey _____ (never be) a model prisoner.

9. In the past year, Joey _____ (write) his mother twice.

10. Joey _____ (seem) very busy in the last few weeks.

PRESENT TENSE REVIEW

DIRECTIONS: Fill in the blanks with the following tenses. In some cases (✔), more than one tense is possible.

SIMPLE PRESENT
PRESENT CONTINUOUS
PRESENT PERFECT
PRESENT PERFECT CONTINUOUS

FRIDAY AFTERNOON AT MacGRUDER'S DEPARTMENT STORE

It's a normal Friday afternoon at MacGruder's Department Store. At this moment in the shoe department, a young man and his wife (1)_____ (try) to buy new shoes for their three small children. The kids (2)_____ (wiggle) and (3)_____ (scream) and (4)_____ (chase) each other around. The salesman, George, (5)_____ ✔ (go) crazy. He (6)_____ ✔ (wait on) the family for the past hour, with no success. Either the shoes (7)_____ (not fit), or the children's father (8)_____ (think) they're too expensive.

Over at the jewelry counter, Julie (9)_____ ✔ (have) a hard time, too. She (10)_____ ✔ (run) back and forth all afternoon. One lady (11)_____ ✔ (try on) earrings for twenty-five minutes and (12)_____ ✔ (not put) them back on the rack, so now there is a mountain of earrings on the counter.

Meanwhile, Beth Ellen, the store detective, (13)_____ ✔ (walk) slowly around the store since she arrived at 10:00. Her feet (14)_____ (kill) her the whole time. Every day, she (15)_____ (walk) around and (16)_____ (try) to look like a normal shopper while she (17)_____ ✔ (do) her job catching shoplifters. Unfortunately, Beth Ellen (18)_____ ✔ (not catch) a single shoplifter in the past year because she can't see well, and she (19)_____ (refuse) to wear her glasses.

Up in his office right now, Mr. MacGruder (20)_____ (stand) by a small window which (21)_____ (look) out over the first floor of his store. He (22)_____ (see) a customer at the jewelry counter secretly putting expensive earrings into her purse. Beth Ellen (23)_____ (walk) right past her at this very moment, but of course she (24)_____ (not see) the woman steal the earrings because she (25)_____ (not wear) her glasses. Mr. MacGruder's face (26)_____ (begin) to turn purple, and now he (27)_____ (tear) out his hair. He (28)_____ ✔ (regret) hiring Beth Ellen as the store detective ever since his sister persuaded him to, but he can't do anything about it because the girl (29)_____ (be) his niece.

DIRECTIONS: Use the phrases and pictures on this page to help you rewrite the story of MacGruder's Department Store. DO NOT LOOK BACK AT THE ORIGINAL STORY. Your story will have four paragraphs—one for each of the pictures below. Your story won't be exactly the same as the original, but you should correctly use the four tenses from this chapter: PRESENT CONTINUOUS, SIMPLE PRESENT, PRESENT PERFECT, and PRESENT PERFECT CONTINUOUS. The verbs on this page are in either picture form or the simple form.

CUE SHEET

1. try to buy
   wiggle/scream/chase
   wait on (for an hour)
   go crazy
   not fit

2. have a hard time
   run back and forth
   try on (for 25 minutes)
   not put back

3. walk slowly
   (since she arrived)
   feet—kill
   try to look like
   not catch a single shoplifter
   refuse to wear

4. stand
   look
   see a customer
   Beth Ellen walk/not see/not wear
   turn purple
   tear out his hair
   regret — since
   the girl be

In the shoe department of MacGruder's Department Store, a man and woman are trying to buy shoes for their kids.

DIRECTIONS: **A.** Use these Story Lines to help you answer the questions on the next page. The verbs on this page are all in the simple form, but you'll choose the correct tenses.

FRIDAY NIGHT

① LEAVE THE STORE

② DRIVE HOME

③ MAKE PLANS FOR THE WEEKEND

① GET TO THE PARTY

② STOP THINKING ABOUT WORK

① BEGIN TO DANCE

① HAVE A GOOD TIME

② DANCE WITH JULIE

③ NOT THINK ABOUT WORK

TAKE A PILL FOR HIS ULCER (4 TIMES A DAY)

LEAVE FOR HIS SISTER'S HOUSE (EVERY FRI.)

① SIT DOWN

② BEGIN TO YELL AT BETH ELLEN

① SIT AT THE DINING TABLE

② YELL

③ SHAKE HIS FINGER AT BETH ELLEN

① TAKE THE BUS (M·T·W·TH·F)

② DREAM ABOUT BEING A FAMOUS DETECTIVE ON T.V. (M·T·W·TH·F ON THE BUS)

GET HOME

BEGIN TO CRY

① SIT ACROSS THE TABLE FROM HER UNCLE

② CRY

③ PROMISE TO WEAR HER GLASSES (EVERY TIME HER UNCLE GETS MAD)

B. Look at the Story Lines on the previous page and answer these questions. Be sure to use the same tenses as in the questions.

1.   What's George doing right now?
2.   How long has he been at the party?
3.   How long has he been off work?
4.   Why is he having a good time?
5.   Has he thought about work this evening? (since/for)
6.   What time does he usually leave work?
7.   When does he make plans for the weekend? (while)
8.   Where is Mr. MacGruder sitting?
9.   What's he doing?
10. How long has he been yelling at Beth Ellen?
11. Why is he yelling at her?
12. How often does he have dinner at his sister's?
13. Why does Mr. MacGruder take pills?
14. How often does he take these pills?
15. Why do you think he has an ulcer?
16. What's Beth Ellen doing? What else?
17. Why is she crying?
18. How long has she been crying?
19. How does she usually get home?
20. What does she do on the bus?
21. How often does she promise to wear her glasses?

IT'S YOUR TURN: Use the PRESENT CONTINUOUS, SIMPLE PRESENT, PRESENT PERFECT, and PRESENT PERFECT CONTINUOUS in the following exercises.

A.   Choose 2 or 3 people (or groups of people) from the list below. Write one paragraph about each. Use your imagination! What are these people doing? What do they usually do? How long have they been doing these things?

a famous movie star	a famous athlete
someone in your family	the president (prime minister,
the people in your country	king, queen) of your country
your teacher	an astronaut

B.   Pretend you are a television news reporter. You're giving a live report from the scene of an event happening right now. Describe the event. Choose one of the following situations/events:

a fashion show	a war zone	a stunt on a movie set
a movie premiere	a flood	a sports event

PAST

5

SIMPLE PAST
PRESENT PERFECT

DIRECTIONS: Read the story on the left. When you finish, go back to the beginning, cover up the story to the left, and choose the correct tense for each capitalized simple form of the verb to the right of the picture.

THE
SNOB

—This is certainly a nice party, isn't it?

—Oh, it's all right, but last week I *attended* an elegant party on the royal yacht.

—Actually, I*'ve been* to so many of these parties lately that they*'ve become* quite a bore.

—Maybe you need a good vacation. *Have* you ever *gone* up to Lake Gorgeous? It's quite nice this year. We*'ve been* there twice.

—This is certainly a nice party, isn't it?

—Oh, it's all right, but last week I ATTEND an elegant party on the royal yacht.

—Actually, I BE to so many of these parties lately that they BECOME quite a bore.

—Maybe you need a good vacation. You ever GO up to Lake Gorgeous? It's quite nice this year. We BE there twice.

—Oh, yes, I know. Our family *has owned* that lake for generations.

—On our last vacation we *spent* most of our time fishing.

—I*'ve* never *liked* fishing, but I*'ve* just *returned* from a shark-hunting trip. I *found* it exciting—well, sort of.

—Speaking of excitement, I*'ve* recently *learned* how to fly a plane.

—Oh, I*'ve* often *flown* our jumbo jet myself. Why, just last week I *flew* it across the Atlantic.

—I*'ve* always *found* swimming a nice way to relax.

—Oh, yes, I know. Our family OWN that lake for generations.

—On our last vacation we SPEND most of our time fishing.

—I never LIKE fishing, but I just RETURN from a shark-hunting trip. I FIND it exciting—well, sort of.

—Speaking of excitement, I recently LEARN how to fly a plane.

—Oh, I often FLY our jumbo jet myself. Why, just last week I FLY it across the Atlantic.

—I always FIND swimming a nice way to relax.

—I've *gotten* tired of swimming. Last year we *went* diving for pearls. That *was* a bit more interesting.

—That reminds me. My husband *bought* me a beautiful string of pearls for my birthday.

—My husband *has* already *bought* me so much jewelry that last April he *decided* to trade it all in on a diamond mine.

—Oh, it *was* in April that we *bought* our new house. It is a roomy four-bedroom place with a swimming pool.

—We've *bought* two homes this year. The first *was* too small; it *had* only 25 rooms.

—The second one is more comfortable. We've just *built* a large indoor swimming pool in addition to the one outside.

—I GET tired of swimming. Last year we GO diving for pearls. That BE a bit more interesting.

—That reminds me. My husband BUY me a beautiful string of pearls for my birthday.

—My husband already BUY me so much jewelry that last April he DECIDE to trade it all in on a diamond mine.

—Oh, it BE in April that we BUY our new house. It is a roomy four-bedroom place with a swimming pool.

—We BUY two homes this year. The first BE too small; it HAVE only 25 rooms.

—The second one is more comfortable. We just BUILD a large indoor swimming pool in addition to the one outside.

—How many rooms *did* you *say* it had?

—I have no idea. I *haven't seen* all of the rooms yet.

I*'ve had* a lot of house guests in the last few months.

—I*'ve* always *enjoyed* the company of good friends.

—Oh, yes, in the past few years I*'ve acquired* a large circle of friends all around the world. My goodness! Where *has* everyone *gone*?

THE END

—How many rooms you SAY it had?

—I have no idea. I NOT SEE all of the rooms yet.

I HAVE a lot of house guests in the last few months.

—I always ENJOY the company of good friends.

—Oh, yes, in the past few years I ACQUIRE a large circle of friends all around the world. My goodness! Where everyone GO?

SIMPLE PAST	PRESENT PERFECT

1.

We use the SIMPLE PAST for a single finished action in the past. The sentence or context often includes such time clues as *yesterday, last week, last year*, or *at 2:30*. These words are not always in the sentence, but they are in the mind of the speaker.

PAST   NOW

Last week I *attended* a party on the royal yacht.

Did you ever *go* up to that lake? (. . . when you lived in Canada)

NOTE: Some people use the SIMPLE PAST instead of the PRESENT PERFECT with time adverbs.

I *didn't see* them yet.
I *already saw* that movie.

This use is less formal and more conversational.

We use the PRESENT PERFECT for a past action when the time of the action isn't known or isn't important. The meaning of the tense in this case is "some time (or any time) *before now*."

NOW

We often use the PRESENT PERFECT with these words:

ever = "at any time in your/his/her (and so on) life" in questions and negative statements.

Have you ever *gone* up to that lake?
He *hasn't* ever *been* on a yacht.

never = "not ever."

She's never *liked* fishing.

yet = "before now" in questions when the activity is expected to have happened. *Yet* is also used in negative statements.

Has she *bought* a house yet?
I *haven't seen* all the rooms yet.

still = "before now" in negative statements. *Still* implies that the activity should have occurred but hasn't.

She still *hasn't seen* all the rooms.

already = "before now" in affirmative statements and in questions. The use of *already* suggests that the activity has happened earlier than expected.

Has she already *gotten* bored?

2.

The SIMPLE PAST can also express a repeated past action. The period of time in which the action happened is also over.

```
      ┌─────────┐       |
  ─────┼×─×─×───┴───────┼──────
            NOW
```

They *went* there several times last year.

The SIMPLE PAST is used with phrases such as *this weekend* and *this year* if, in the speaker's mind, the time is finished. In December, a person uses the PAST with *this year* because in his mind the year is finished.

I *went* there twice this year.

The PRESENT PERFECT expresses one action (or the repetition of an action) that is finished. However, the period of time in which it happened is not over.

```
           ┌─────────┐
  ─────────┼─×─×─×──┴|────────
                NOW
```

They*'ve gone* there several times this year.

This unfinished period of time may be *this week* (weekend, month, year), *today*, or others. Sometimes this period of time is quite long: *in the past ten years, in my life*, and so on. The indication of time (*this year* and so on) is not always in the sentence; it is often only in the mind of the speaker/writer.

I*'ve been* there twice. (in my life)

3.

The SIMPLE PAST is also used for a finished activity of duration.

```
      ┌─────────┐     |
  ─────┴─────────┴─────┼──────
            NOW
```

Our family *owned* that lake for generations. (We don't own it now.)

The PRESENT PERFECT is used for an action happening now when we have some idea of when the action began or how long it has gone on.

```
      |        ⌒         ▸·─·
  ────┴────────────────────────
              NOW
```

Our family *has owned* that lake for generations. (We own it now.)

For more on this use of the PRESENT PERFECT, see Chapter 2.

4.

The SIMPLE PAST is used with certain verbs to express the *beginning* of an action.

Some of these verbs are:

find out ─────────────▸ know
meet ─────────────────▸ know
get (become) ─────────▸ be

The PRESENT PERFECT is used with certain other verbs to express the duration or continuation of an activity that was begun in the past.

Some of these verbs are:

get (receive, buy, obtain) ——————→	have
go to bed ——————————————→	sleep
learn ——————————————————→	know
put on ——————————————————→	wear
pick up —————————————————→	hold
catch (a cold) ———————————→	have (a cold)
join (a club) ———————————→	belong to (a club)
He *put on* that cap this morning. ——→	He's *worn* that cap all day.
I *learned* how to drive when I was a——→	I've *known* how to drive since I was a
teenager.	teenager.
She *caught* a cold last week. ————→	She's *had* a cold for a week.
They *got* married in 1960.————————→	They've *been* married a long time.

5.   Both the SIMPLE PAST and the PRESENT PERFECT are used with a very recently completed action, but the PRESENT PERFECT is more common.

I just *finished.*	I've just *finished.*
They *bought* a lot of land recently.	They've *bought* a lot of land recently.

RAP IT UP

DIRECTIONS: **A.** Work with a partner. Ask and answer questions about the people in the pictures. For each of the items below the pictures ask two questions (ever/yet). Use the time expression in the answer.

Examples: —Has she ever flown a plane?   —Has she flown a plane yet?
               —Yes, she flew one last year.   —Yes, she flew one last year.

1. fly a plane/last year
2. attend a party/last week
3. buy a string of pearls/last February
4. swim across the English Channel/ many years ago
5. drive a sports car/never

6. jog/yesterday
7. spend time in Acapulco/in 1982
8. lie on the Riviera/never
9. lend money to someone/in July
10. ride a camel/never

B. Work with a partner. Ask and answer "how often" questions. Use a verb and a time expression from the lists below.

Examples: —How often has she (have they) flown this year?
—She's (they've) flown 3 times this year.
—How often did she (did they) fly last year?
—She (they) flew 20 times last year.

VERBS AND VERB PHRASES

fly, go fishing, go shark hunting, climb mountains, dive for pearls, ski, dine out, give a party, hike, take a cruise, sail around the world, sell stocks, bet money at the races, consult a gypsy, go on a safari, peel potatoes, buy a house

---

TIME EXPRESSIONS

today	yesterday
this year	last year
this month	last month
this week	last week
this weekend	last weekend

C. Work with a partner. Ask and answer questions about Regina and Oscar using the chart below.

Examples: —When did she buy a car?
—She bought one in 1980.
—Does she still own the car?
—Yes, she's owned it since 1980.

—When did they buy a boat?
—They bought one in 1975.
—Do they still own the boat?
—No, they owned it for 5 years, but they don't anymore.

1975	1980	last year	now

buy a car --- own a car
buy a boat ------------------- own a boat
   join a yacht club--belong to a yacht club
borrow money------------------------------------- owe money
   find out our address------------------------------------know our address
   get sick ------------------------- get well
become a doctor --- be a doctor
buy a house--own a house
   get married---be married

D. Work with a partner. Ask your partner as many questions as possible using the pictures below and a time expression from the list. Use the SIMPLE PAST or PRESENT PERFECT tense.

Examples: —Have you been in a car crash this year?
                —No, I haven't.

                —Were you in a car crash last year?
                —No, I wasn't.

> **TIME EXPRESSIONS**
>
> | | | |
> |---|---|---|
> | ever | in 1979 | today |
> | last month | 4 years ago | yet |
> | this year | in the past week | already |
> | May | never | just |

PICTURE PUZZLE

DIRECTIONS: On another piece of paper, write out the following story. Change all of the pictures and symbols to words. For each of the encircled verbs, choose the SIMPLE PAST or the PRESENT PERFECT. In a few cases, more than one tense may be possible. The characters are Oscar and Regina. (Regina was the woman from the story earlier in this chapter.) Use pronouns whenever possible. If you can't guess the meaning of a symbol, check page 163 in the Appendix.

Oscar is a rich man, but he has a lot of problems. What are some of them?

THE CAUSE OF OSCAR'S ULCER

{} 'S WIFE, REGINA, (DRIVE) {} CRAZY FOR YEARS. ⊡ THEIR WEDDING ☼ , {}{}

(SWEAR) → STICK TOGETHER FOREVER, BUT THE ROMANCE (DIE) SOON AFTER THE HONEY-

MOON.

{} (ALWAYS BE) RICH, BUT {} (NEVER BE) INTERESTED ☒ HIS 💵 . {} (ALWAYS WANT)

A SIMPLE LIFE. BEFORE 🧔 (GET) MARRIED, 🧔 (LIKE) → GO CAMPING. 🧔 OFTEN (GO) HIKING ↑ ☒ THE 〰️s. 🧔 (SIT) ☐☒ A STREAM ☒ THE SHADE OF A BIG 🌳 OR (LIE) ☒ A HAMMOCK FOR HOURS. 📅 WEEK ENDS, 🧔 (LIKE) → STAY 🏠 & MOW THE LAWN.

HOWEVER. 🧔'S LIFE (BE) VERY DIFFERENT SINCE HIS MARRIAGE. 🧔 & 👩 (GO) 📅 FOUR CRUISES 🔲 THE 🌍 ☒ THE PAST FIVE YEARS. 👩 (INSIST) 📅 🧔 BUYING 👩 SO MUCH 💎 THAT LAST APRIL 🧔 (GIVE) ↑ & (BUY) 👩 A 💍 MINE. 👩 (WITHDRAW) ⅓ OF THE 💵 ☒ THEIR BANK ACCOUNT LAST YEAR, & 👩 (WITHDRAW) ANOTHER ⅓ THIS YEAR.

RECENTLY, THE SITUATION (GET) EVEN WORSE. LAST MONTH, 👩 (TEAR) ↑ THE LAWN ☒ THE BACKYARD & (TEAR) ↓ 🧔'S HAMMOCK. AFTER THAT, 👩 (THROW) 🔲→ HIS FAVORITE 🎣ING 🐟, HIKING 👢s, & ⛺.

🧔 (HAVE) AN ULCER FOR YEARS. HIS DOCTOR (OFTEN TELL) 🧔 → TAKE IT EASY & → STOP 🍔ING & 🥤ING. BUT 🧔 & 👩 (JUST RECENTLY FIND) A SOLUTION → BOTH 🧔'S ULCER & THEIR MARRIAGE PROBLEMS. LAST WEEK, 👩 (AGREE) → GO 🎣ING W/ 🧔 ↑ ☒ THE 〰️s. ☒ RETURN, 🧔 (AGREE) → BUY 👩 A MINK 🏔. 🧔👩 (GO) 📅 THEIR 🎣ING TRIP & (HAVE) A GREAT TIME. 🧔👩 (A̶R̶G̶U̶E̶) ABOUT ANYTHING SINCE THEN.

PAST CONTINUOUS
SIMPLE PAST

DIRECTIONS: Read the story on the left. When you finish, go back to the beginning, cover up the story to the left, and choose the correct tense for each capitalized simple form of the verb to the right of the picture.

—This is Douglas Jones, WBC News. I'm talking to little Jimmy Anderson who has an amazing story to tell. Jimmy, can you tell us what *happened* yesterday afternoon?

—We *were having* a normal Sunday afternoon when something unbelievable *happened*.

Dad *was mowing* the lawn while Mom *was fixing* the car.

My sister, Lucy, *was peeling* potatoes and *making* a salad.

—This is Douglas Jones, WBC News. I'm talking to little Jimmy Anderson who has an amazing story to tell. Jimmy, can you tell us what HAPPEN yesterday afternoon?

—We HAVE a normal Sunday afternoon when something unbelievable HAPPEN.

Dad MOW the lawn while Mom FIX the car.

My sister, Lucy, PEEL potatoes and MAKE a salad.

My brother, Harold, *was sleeping* in the shade of the big oak tree that afternoon.

My younger sister, Sally, and her friend *were playing* ball when the commotion *began*.

I *was trying* to teach my dog, Rusty, how to shake hands (without much success) when he *began* to growl.

Even the cat, Jasmine, who *was licking* her paws, suddenly *stopped*.

I *was trying* to figure out what *was happening* when a strange object *came* down from the sky.

It *floated* down and *landed* right in our backyard while we *were* all *standing* there watching.

My brother, Harold, SLEEP in the shade of the big oak tree that afternoon.

My younger sister, Sally, and her friend PLAY ball when the commotion BEGIN.

I TRY to teach my dog, Rusty, how to shake hands (without much success) when he BEGIN to growl.

Even the cat, Jasmine, who LICK her paws, suddenly STOP.

I TRY to figure out what HAPPEN when a strange object COME down from the sky.

It FLOAT down and LAND right in our backyard while we all STAND there watching.

At first everyone *was* too afraid to move. Then we slowly *approached* the object.

We *were standing* around the object, hardly breathing, when suddenly a door *opened*.

When the door *opened*, we all *took* a step back.

Everyone *was waiting* anxiously when two little green creatures *came* out of the door.

When one of the creatures *raised* its hands, Sally *fainted*. Her friend *screamed* and *ran* into the house.

My knees *were shaking* when the creatures *stepped* onto the lawn.

At first everyone BE too afraid to move. Then we slowly APPROACH the object.

We STAND around the object, hardly breathing, when suddenly a door OPEN.

When the door OPEN we all TAKE a step back.

Everyone WAIT anxiously when two little green creatures COME out of the door.

When one of the creatures RAISE its hands, Sally FAINT. Her friend SCREAM and RUN into the house.

My knees SHAKE when the creatures STEP onto the lawn.

Harold *was* still *sleeping* under the tree.

Harold still SLEEP under the tree.

The two creatures *were looking* us *over* when suddenly Rusty *ran* out from under Harold's hammock.

The two creatures LOOK us OVER when suddenly Rusty RUN out from under Harold's hammock.

When Rusty *saw* the creatures, he *started* to bark.

When Rusty SEE the creatures, he START to bark.

When the creatures *heard*. . .

When the creatures HEAR. . .

—Oh, there you are, Jimmy! I *was looking* for you. Come home now. It's time for dinner. You *weren't making up* space stories again, *were* you?

—Oh, there you are, Jimmy! I LOOK for you. Come home now. It's time for dinner. You NOT MAKE UP space stories again, (—) you?

THE END

PAST CONTINUOUS	SIMPLE PAST

1. The PAST CONTINUOUS is used for an action in progress at a specific time in the past.

My brother *was sleeping* at 2:00 yesterday afternoon. (He went to sleep sometime before 2:00 and continued sleeping after 2:00.)

See Chapter 5 for several uses of the SIMPLE PAST.

2. The PAST CONTINUOUS is used for a past action that was in progress when another action happened. The verb in the PAST CONTINUOUS may stop when the second action occurs, or it may continue beyond the second action.

We *were having* a normal Sunday afternoon when something unbelievable happened. (We stopped having a normal afternoon.)

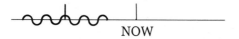

My knees *were shaking* when the creatures stepped onto the lawn. (My knees continued shaking.)

Note that the PAST CONTINUOUS is not an independent tense. It is used with *another time* in either the sentence or context.

The SIMPLE PAST is used for the action that interrupts (or happens during) the PAST CONTINUOUS action. When the SIMPLE PAST and PAST CONTINUOUS are in the same sentence, the SIMPLE PAST is usually the shorter action.

When both actions are in the SIMPLE PAST, the meaning is not the same as it is when one tense is PAST CONTINUOUS.

We *were eating* when he got here. (He got here during our dinner.)

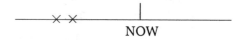

We *ate* when he got here. (He got here, and then we ate.)

3. When two actions in the past happen at the same time and we emphasize the duration of each action, we use the PAST CONTINUOUS for both.

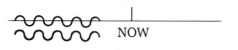

	Dad *was moving* the lawn while Mom *was fixing* the car.	
4.	The PAST CONTINUOUS is often used in clauses with *while* and *as*. Dad *was mowing* the lawn while Mom *was fixing* the car. (no comma) While Dad *was mowing* the lawn, Mom *was fixing* the car. (comma) *While* and *as* both mean *when* in a continuous sense. They are usually used before a continuous tense. But sometimes the PAST CONTINUOUS is used after *when*.	After *when*, the verb is usually in a simple tense such as the SIMPLE PAST. We were all standing around the object when suddenly a door *opened*. The SIMPLE PAST can also be used after *while* and *as*. When it is, the meaning is continuous. While we *watched* in horror, the strange object landed.
5.	The PAST CONTINUOUS is not used with verbs that have NON-ACTION meanings. (See the Appendix, page 155.)	The SIMPLE PAST is used for NON-ACTION verbs even when the meaning is of duration. (See the Appendix, page 155.)
6.	The PAST CONTINUOUS sometimes expresses repetition in the past. I *was coughing* all night long. When the PAST CONTINUOUS is used with *always*, *forever*, or *constantly*, it expresses a frequent activity in the past about which we feel some emotion (irritation, amusement, admiration, and so on). We *were* forever *getting* into trouble. He *was* always *asking* questions.	The SIMPLE PAST can also express repetition in the past. I *coughed* all night long. *Always* is used with the SIMPLE PAST for habitual actions in the past. I always *got up* at 6:00 when I was in high school. It is also used for a past condition. She always *liked* animals.
7.	We use the PAST CONTINUOUS in indirect speech when the direct quote is in the PRESENT CONTINUOUS. "My brother *is talking* to a reporter," she said. = She said her brother *was talking* to a reporter.	We use the SIMPLE PAST in indirect speech when the direct quote is in the SIMPLE PRESENT. "He often *talks* to reporters," she said. = She said he often *talked* to reporters.

DIRECTIONS: **A.** Work with a partner. Make up as many logical sentences as you can using combinations of any two of the pictures below. Use the SIMPLE PAST and the PAST CONTINUOUS tenses.

Examples: Dad *was sneezing* while he *was mowing* the lawn.
The space creature *was doing* experiments when the fire *broke* out.

B. Use the SIMPLE PAST and the PAST CONTINUOUS tenses. Make up at least ten sentences for each part (1 and 2).

1. Imagine that a spaceship landed on your street last Saturday. Tell what you, your friends, family, neighbors, and so on, were doing at the time and what happened.

2. Tell about an unusual event in your life. Describe what you and others were doing at the time and what happened. Examples of events: a traffic accident, an earthquake, a fire, and so on.

DIRECTIONS: Fill in the blanks in the following story with the SIMPLE PAST or PAST CONTINUOUS. Remember that more than one tense may be possible in some of the blanks.

A STRANGE DAY ON PLANET ZENON

This is XR 101, Planet Zenon News. I'm talking to little TQ005 who has an amazing story to tell. TQ, can you tell us what (1)_____ (happen) yesterday?

We (2)_____ (have) a normal Sunday afternoon when something unbelievable (3)_____ (happen). Dad (4)_____ (dig) craters in the backyard while Mom (5)_____ (punch) our dinner order into the computer. My sister, RQ005, (6)_____ (check) the computer printout to make sure it (7)_____ (match) what Mom (8)_____ (order). My brother, PQ005, (9)_____ (repair) his rocket. My younger sister, VQ005, and her friend (10)_____ (do) experiments in her laboratory when the trouble (11)_____ (begin).

I (12)_____ (oil) my robot when suddenly it (13)_____ (sound) its warning alarm. When the alarm (14)_____ (begin) to ring, everyone (15)_____ (stop) what they (16)_____ (do). We (17)_____ (try) to find out why the alarm (18)_____ (ring) when a strange object (19)_____ (appear) in the sky. It (20)_____ (seem) to be coming directly toward us. And in a few minutes, it (21)_____ (land) right in Dad's newly made crater. We all (22)_____ (hold) our breath. While we (23)_____ (watch), one of the doors slowly (24)_____ (open). Then two of the ugliest creatures I've ever seen (25)_____ (step) into the doorway. I (26)_____ (hide) my eyes from the horrible sight when they (27)_____ (begin) coming closer. The robot (28)_____ (begin) to examine them as they (29)_____ (approach). When the robot's arm (30)_____ (reach) out to grab them, the two creatures (31)_____ (run) back into their ship and (32)_____ (begin) to take off again. As the ship (33)_____ (climb) back up to the sky, I (34)_____ (see) the strange markings on the side that (35)_____ (look) like this: "Planet Earth."

DIRECTIONS: Read the story on the left. When you finish, go back to the beginning, cover up the story to the left, and choose the correct tense for each capitalized simple form of the verb to the right of the picture.

When I *was* young, I used to dream about my future.

When I BE young, I used to dream about my future.

I *dreamed* that I *was going to be* a famous rock star.

I DREAM that I BE a famous rock star.

I *thought* people *were going to chase* me down the street, begging me for my autograph.

I THINK people CHASE me down the street, begging me for my autograph.

I *thought* that everyone *would know* me and that I *would wear* sunglasses to hide.

I THINK that everyone KNOW me and that I WEAR sunglasses to hide.

Because I *was going to be* rich, I *knew* I *was going to have* a big, beautiful house with a huge swimming pool.

I *dreamed* I *would be able* to jet to Paris for lunch.

I *thought* that I *was going to spend* my summers lying on a beach on the French Riviera.

Kings and queens *would become* my friends.

Thousands of rich, beautiful women *would beg* me to marry them.

But I always *said* that I *was going to be* kind and generous to those people not as lucky as I was.

Because I BE rich, I KNOW I HAVE a big, beautiful house with a huge swimming pool.

I DREAM I BE ABLE to jet to Paris for lunch.

I THINK that I SPEND my summers lying on a beach on the French Riviera.

Kings and queens BECOME my friends.

Thousands of rich, beautiful women BEG me to marry them.

But I always SAY that I BE kind and generous to those people not as lucky as I was.

I *knew* everyone *was going to know* and *love* me.

I KNOW everyone KNOW and LOVE me.

However, success *did* not *come* to me easily. There *were* many times I *thought* I *would* never *become* a rock star.

However, success NOT COME to me easily. There BE many times I THINK I never BECOME a rock star.

I *was going to become* a famous rock star, but in the beginning, I *did*n't *know* the right people. So for a time, I *was* a street-corner musician.

I BECOME a famous rock star, but in the beginning, I NOT KNOW the right people. So for a time, I BE a street-corner musician.

No one *knew* me, and only dogs *chased* me down the street.

No one KNOW me, and only dogs CHASE me down the street.

My home *was* a bench in the park, and the only pools *were* made by the rain.

My home BE a bench in the park, and the only pools BE made by the rain.

Sometimes I *got away* for lunch, but I never *went* far.

Sometimes I GET AWAY for lunch, but I never GO far.

I *spent* my summers trying to keep cool.

My friends *were* not kings and queens.

Women hardly *noticed* me.

But I still *tried* to help others as much as I could.

I *was* not famous, but to my friends, I *was* a great star.

THE END

I SPEND my summers trying to keep cool.

My friends BE not kings and queens.

Women hardly NOTICE me.

But I still TRY to help others as much as I could.

I BE not famous, but to my friends, I BE a great star.

FUTURE IN THE PAST	SIMPLE PAST

1.

The FUTURE IN THE PAST is used for an action that was intended but never happened.	In this use of the FUTURE IN THE PAST, the SIMPLE PAST is used for the reason *why* the intended action didn't happen.
I *was going to become* a rock star, but I didn't know the right people in the music business.	I was going to become a rock star, but I *didn't know* the right people.

2.

The *was/were going to* form is also used in noun clauses that are the direct object of a PAST TENSE verb. In this way, it expresses an action that we thought (said, dreamed, and so on) would happen at some time *after* the time we thought it.

NOW

dreamed   was going to become
(At some time "future
from" the time
I dreamed.)

I dreamed (that) I *was going to become* a famous rock star.

In this use, *was/were going to (become)* has the same meaning as *would (become)*.

I dreamed (that) I *would become* a famous rock star.

In these clauses, the word *that* is optional.

A SIMPLE PAST verb from one of the following two groups occurs before a noun clause with *would (verb)* or *was/were going to (verb)*.

VERBS OF MENTAL ACTIVITY such as

believed	hoped
decided	imagined
doubted	knew
dreamed	predicted
felt	pretended
found out	realized
forgot	remembered
guessed	thought
had no idea	was/were sure

and

VERBS OF INDIRECT SPEECH such as

announced	reported
boasted	said
complained	told (someone)
explained	swore
mentioned	

I *knew* (that) I was going to have a big house with a pool.

I always *said* (that) I would be kind and generous to everyone.

DIRECTIONS: **A.** Column 1 below is a list of activities that Frankie and his brother wanted to do. Column 2 gives reasons why they never did them. Make as many sentences as possible combining an item from Column 1 with one from Column 2. Many combinations are possible, but make sure they are logical.

Examples: They were going to go fishing, but the car broke down.
                 They were going to go fishing, but they were too tired.

Column 1	Column 2
go to the movies	can't sing
call home	forget
go on a picnic	it was too hot
take photographs	be too afraid
mow the lawn	not have a car/fishing pole/film/and so on
become artists	get sick
buy their mother earrings	not have enough money
go fishing	have to take care of their baby sister
go mountain climbing	it rained
become famous singers	be too tired
go to the circus	lawn mower break/car break down/and so on
buy a newspaper	decide not to
play chess	lose crayons
go shark hunting	
join the school chorus	
make posters	

B. Work with another student. Make up as many sentences as you can about the following pictures. Use the SIMPLE PAST and the FUTURE IN THE PAST.

Examples: When Frankie was a child, he thought he was going to become a pilot.
                 He was sure he would fly around the world.

C. Work with a partner. Tell about things you expected or intended that turned out differently. Make up at least 10 sentences using the SIMPLE PAST and the FUTURE IN THE PAST.

Examples: Before I came to this country, I thought all the cities were going to be large.
I was going to call you, but I forgot.

PICTURE PUZZLE

DIRECTIONS: On another piece of paper, write out the following story, changing all of the pictures and symbols to words. The character's name is Frankie, but you should use pronouns (he, him) whenever possible. For each of the encircled verbs, choose the PAST TENSE or the FUTURE IN THE PAST. If you can't guess the meaning of a symbol, check page 163 in the Appendix.

A DAY IN THE LIFE OF A STREET MUSICIAN

(WAKE) ↑ 1 ☀ LAST YEAR & (DECIDE) THAT IT (BE) A GOOD DAY FOR . (PICK) ↑ HIS 🎸 & (GO) → HIS USUAL PLACE ⊠ THE 🌳. (PUT) ↓ HIS 🎸 CASE & (BEGIN) → PLAY. (BE) SURE A LOT OF 👥 (COME) → LISTEN → PLAY.

AT **1**ST, THE 🌳 (BE) VERY QUIET. THERE (BE) ONLY A FEW 🐿s & 🐦s WHO (COME) → BECAUSE THEY (THINK) (GIVE) THEM SOMETHING → EAT. THEN A LOT OF 👥 (BEGIN) → RUSH → ⏠ THEIR WAY → WORK, BUT (KNOW) THEY (P~~U~~T) ANY 💵 ⊠ HIS 🎸 CASE BECAUSE 👥 (BE) ⊠ A HURRY.

(PLAY) ALL A.M. & (THINK) ABOUT HIS FUTURE. (KNOW) THAT (BE~~C~~OME) A FAMOUS 🎤♪ ⊠ THE FUTURE. (REALIZE) THAT (NEVER HAVE) A BIG 🏠 W/ A ____ING ____. (KNOW) THAT HE (NEVER BE ABLE) → BUY AN $↑ 🚗. (BE SURE) THAT (NEVER TRAVEL) (□↑ THE 🌍 ⏠ A 🚢. (BEGIN) → FEEL REALLY ☹.

AT ABOUT 🕔, A POLICEWOMAN (COME) →. FOR A MINUTE, (BE) AFRAID THAT SHE (ARREST) (OR AT LEAST (CHASE) OUT OF THE 🌳) FOR PLAYING W/OUT A PERMIT. BUT THE POLICEWOMAN JUST (STOP), (SIT) ↓ ⏠ A 🪑, & (LISTEN) → . AFTER A FEW MINUTES, THE POLICEWOMAN (GET) ↑, (PUT) SOME 💵 ⊠ 's 🎸 CASE, & (SAY), "YOU PLAY VERY WELL!"

THEN THE POLICEWOMAN (TELL) THAT SHE (HAVE) A BROTHER WHO (WORK) FOR A [radio] STATION [x] ANOTHER CITY. SHE (SAY) SHE (TALK) W/ HIM [on] THE [telephone] LATER THAT

[sun] & THAT SHE (ASK) HER BROTHER → HAVE [him] PLAY HIS [guitar] [on] HIS [radio] PROGRAM.

WELL, OF COURSE [he] (BE) THRILLED. [he] (BEGIN) → DREAM THAT MAYBE [he] REALLY

(BECOME) A FAMOUS [musician] MAYBE [he] (BE ABLE) → BUY A BIG [house] & AN $[up] [car].

MAYBE [he] (TRAVEL) ([around]) THE [world] [on] A [ship]. MAYBE...

RECAP

DIRECTIONS: Fill in the blanks with the following tenses. In some cases, more than one tense may be possible.

SIMPLE PAST
PRESENT PERFECT
PAST CONTINUOUS
FUTURE IN THE PAST (*would* or *be going to* + simple form)

GREAT-AUNT BERTHA VS. THE CITY COUNCIL

My Great-Aunt Bertha is 95 years old, and she lives alone in a big old house on Kingsley Drive, where she (1)_____ (live) for over sixty years. In the past decade, we (2)_____ (try) many times to persuade her to move in with us, but she's a very cranky, stubborn lady; she (3)_____ (be) quite independent all her life, so she's quite happy living there with only her five dogs for company.

Well, last month the city council (4)_____ (decide) that they (5)_____ (build) a parking lot on her property. They (6)_____ (send) an eviction notice saying that they (7)_____ (buy) her house and tear it down, so she (8)_____ (have to) move. Aunt Bertha was absolutely furious. She (9)_____ (tell) them that she (10)_____ (not move) anywhere. The Great Battle (11)_____ (begin).

The city (12)_____ (send) a big truck and two very large, strong movers to move my aunt and her household. When the movers (13)_____ (get) there, they (14)_____ (find) that my aunt (15)_____ (sit) in her rocking chair, blocking the doorway. They (16)_____ (wonder) what to do when her five dogs (17)_____ (appear) and (18)_____ (chase) them off.

While the movers (19)_____ (scream) and (20)_____ (run) around the yard, some reporters (21)_____ (arrive) from the local newspaper and from WTTV news. The reporters (22)_____ (take) one look around and (23)_____ (start) to laugh. One of the movers (24)_____ (hide) in his truck as one of the dogs (25)_____ (make) sure that he stayed there. The other mover, up in an elm tree, (26)_____ (cling) to one of the branches while a second dog (27)_____ (growl) at him from below. The reporters (28)_____ (sit) down and (29)_____ (ask) Aunt Bertha what in the world (30)_____ (happen).

That night Aunt Bertha (31)_____ (appear) on the evening news and in the "Daily Herald." She soon (32)_____ (become) famous. The people of the city (33)_____ (be) quite angry with the city council. The council members finally (34)_____ (decide) that they (35)_____ (not build) the parking lot on my aunt's property, after all. My aunt (36)_____ (be) so happy about this news that she (37)_____ (throw) a huge party and invited everyone—even the movers and the city council!

Aunt Bertha (38)_____ (be) very pleased ever since then, and we (39)_____ (notice) a change in her. She (40)_____ (become) less cranky!

DIRECTIONS: Use the phrases and pictures on this page to help you rewrite the story of Great-Aunt Bertha. DO NOT LOOK BACK AT THE ORIGINAL STORY. Your story won't be exactly the same as the original, but you should correctly use the four tenses from this unit. The verbs on this page are in either picture form or the simple form, but you will choose from the following tenses when you rewrite the story on the next page: SIMPLE PAST, PRESENT PERFECT, PAST CONTINUOUS, and FUTURE IN THE PAST (*was/were going to* or *would*).

CUE SHEET

1. try to persuade her to move
   cranky, stubborn
   be independent (all her life)

2. city council—decide/build
   send an eviction notice
   buy/tear down her house
   have to move
   tell them/not move
   Great Battle

3. city—send a big truck
   movers—find my aunt
   wonder
   5 dogs—appear/chase
   movers—scream/run
   reporters—arrive
   mover—hide/cling
   dog—growl
   reporters—sit down/ask

4. Aunt Bertha—appear
   become famous
   people—be angry
   city council—decide/not build
   aunt—be happy/throw a party

5. be pleased since then
   we—notice a change
   she—become

My Aunt Bertha is very old. She
lives alone on Kingsley Drive, where she

DIRECTIONS: A. Use this Story Line to answer the questions on the next page.

AUNT BERTHA'S LIFE

1890
- BERTHA WAS BORN
- FAMILY LIVED ON A FARM IN VERMONT

1895
- SHE LEARNED TO MILK A COW AND FEED CHICKENS

1896
- BEGAN SCHOOL

1899
1. DECIDED TO BECOME A DANCER
2. HER PARENTS PLANNED FOR HER TO BECOME A FARMER'S WIFE

1908
1. GRADUATED FROM HIGH SCHOOL (JUNE 2)
2. GOT ON A TRAIN TO SAN FRANCISCO (JUNE 3)
3. MET JULIAN (A FARMER) ON THE TRAIN
4. FOUND A JOB IN A DRESS SHOP IN SAN FRANCISCO

1909
5. BEGAN DANCE LESSONS (NIGHTS)
6. JULIAN BOUGHT A FARM OUTSIDE SAN FRANCISCO

1. JULIAN PROPOSED MARRIAGE
2. BERTHA SAID "NO"
3. SHE CONTINUED HER DANCE LESSONS

1911
1. SHE TRIED TO GET A JOB AS A DANCER
2. ALL OF THE THEATERS SAID "NO"

1. JULIAN SOLD THE FARM
2. JULIAN PROPOSED MARRIAGE
3. BERTHA SAID "YES"

1912
4. THEY MOVED TO LOS ANGELES
5. JULIAN BOUGHT A SHOP

1913
1. THEY BOUGHT A SMALL HOUSE
2. BERTHA BEGAN GIVING DANCE LESSONS
3. SHE BROKE HER ARM DURING A DANCE LESSON

1915
- HAD A BABY GIRL

1920
1. THEY BOUGHT A HOUSE ON KINGSLEY DRIVE
2. BERTHA PLANNED TO OPEN HER OWN DANCE SCHOOL IN 1921

1921
1. HAD A BABY BOY
2. DIDN'T OPEN A DANCE SCHOOL
3. PLANNED FOR HER DAUGHTER TO BECOME A DANCER

1933
1. HER DAUGHTER GRADUATED FROM HIGH SCHOOL
2. HER DAUGHTER GOT ON A TRAIN TO OHIO
3. HER DAUGHTER MARRIED A FARMER

1940
1. JULIAN DIED OF A HEART ATTACK WHILE ON A PLANE TO N.Y.
2. BERTHA REFUSED EVER TO GET ON A PLANE

1941
- BERTHA BOUGHT A DANCE STUDIO AND HIRED DANCE TEACHERS

NOW
- STILL LIVES ON KINGSLEY DR.
- GOES TO THE BALLET OFTEN

B. Look at the Story Line on the previous page and answer these questions. Be sure to use the same tenses as in the questions.

1. Where was Bertha's family living when she began school?
2. What did she learn to do in 1895?
3. In 1899, what did she decide she was going to become?
4. What did her parents think she was going to become?
5. What did she do right after graduation from school?
6. Where was she going when she met Julian?
7. Where was she working while she was taking dance lessons?
8. Why do you think she said "no" to Julian's proposal?
9. What was she going to become?
10. Why did she change her mind and accept his proposal?
11. Where did they move, and what happened there?
12. What was Bertha doing when she broke her arm?
13. What was she going to open?
14. What did she hope her daughter would become when she grew up?
15. What was Julian doing when he died?
16. How long has she lived on Kingsley Drive?
17. How many cities has she lived in?
18. How long has she been interested in dancing?
19. How many houses has she owned?
20. Has she ever ridden on a train?
21. Has she ever flown on an airplane?

IT'S YOUR TURN: Practice the SIMPLE PAST, PRESENT PERFECT, PAST CONTINUOUS, and FUTURE IN THE PAST (*was/were going to* or *would*) in the following exercises.

A. HOMEWORK: Draw a Story Line with major events in your own life or the life of someone in your family. It probably won't have as many events as Bertha's has, but you should try to have as many events and plans as possible.

B. CLASSWORK: Bring your Story Line to class. Briefly tell another student about it. Then exchange your Story Line with another student's. Ask and answer questions about the details of each other's lives, using the Story Line as a basis.

Examples: —Why did your parents hope you would become a doctor?
—Doctors are respected a lot in my country.
—Why did you want to become a journalist?
—I've always been interested in writing and in traveling. I thought I'd be able to do both as a journalist.

—What part of Hong Kong were you living in when you started school?
—We were living in Kowloon, near the railroad.
—How did you get to school each day?
—I walked. Sometimes I took the bus.

DIRECTIONS: Read the story on the left. When you finish, go back to the beginning, cover up the story to the left, and choose the correct tense for each capitalized simple form of the verb to the right of the picture.

Sam and Charlie *decided* to go on a hike last Saturday.

Sam and Charlie DECIDE to go on a hike last Saturday.

Sam *drove* over and *picked up* Charlie because Charlie's car *had broken down*.

Sam DRIVE over and PICK UP Charlie because Charlie's car BREAK DOWN.

Sam *had had* his driver's license for only two weeks, so he *was* a little nervous.

Sam HAVE his driver's license for only two weeks, so he BE a little nervous.

But they finally *got* to the mountains.

But they finally GET to the mountains.

Charlie *said* that he *had found* a beautiful trail a few weeks earlier.

He *had followed* it up to a lake. . .

. . .but he *hadn't gone* swimming because of the cold water.

So on Saturday, Charlie *led* the way.

Sam *had* some trouble keeping up with him.

They *got* very thirsty because they *had forgotten* to bring something to drink.

Charlie SAY that he FIND a beautiful trail a few weeks earlier.

He FOLLOW it up to a lake. . .

. . .but he NOT GO swimming because of the cold water.

So on Saturday, Charlie LEAD the way.

Sam HAVE some trouble keeping up with him.

They GET very thirsty because they FORGET to bring something to drink.

Finally, they *reached* the lake and *sat* down on a rock to rest.

Charlie *was* hungry because he *hadn't brought* his lunch.

Sam *was* hungry because he *had fed* his sandwich to animals along the trail.

Their feet *hurt* so much that they almost *couldn't move*.

On the way back down the mountain, they *lost* the trail.

By the time they *got* home, the sun *had set*, and it *was* dark.

Finally, they REACH the lake and SIT down on a rock to rest.

Charlie BE hungry because he NOT BRING his lunch.

Sam BE hungry because he FEED his sandwich to animals along the trail.

Their feet HURT so much that they almost CANNOT MOVE.

On the way back down the mountain, they LOSE the trail.

By the time they GET home, the sun SET and it BE dark.

A bee *had stung* Sam. . .

A bee STING Sam. . .

. . .a snake *had bitten* Charlie. . .

...a snake BITE Charlie...

. . .and both of them *had frozen* in the lake.

. . .and both of them FREEZE in the lake.

They *were* very glad to be home.

They BE very glad to be home.

They both *decided* never to go hiking again.

They both DECIDE never to go hiking again.

THE END

PAST PERFECT	SIMPLE PAST
1. We use the PAST PERFECT when we speak or write in the PAST TENSE and then "jump back" to an earlier action.  PAST PAST NOW PERFECT He was hungry because he *hadn't eaten* breakfast. This "jump" can be any length of time—years, months, days, or even minutes.	We usually use the SIMPLE PAST if we move *forward* in time (toward the present) and if it is clear which action happened first. However, in casual conversation, some people don't use the PAST PERFECT, even when they "jump back" in time. Instead, they use the SIMPLE PAST. He was hungry because he *didn't eat* breakfast.
2. In a story, we often jump back and forth from the SIMPLE PAST to the PAST PERFECT. The story at the beginning of this chapter is an illustration of this. 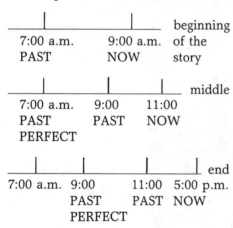	
3. We often use the PAST PERFECT in sentences with adverbial clauses beginning with *until, before, after, when, because,* and *although.* Although Charlie *had been* there a few weeks earlier, he lost the trail on the way home. (comma)	With *before* and *after,* the PAST PERFECT is not always used. It isn't necessary because the time is clear. Instead, we may use the SIMPLE PAST. Sam *had grabbed* his camera before he left. (correct) Sam *grabbed* his camera before he left. (also correct)

Charlie lost the trail on the way home although he *had been* there a few weeks earlier. (no comma)

It's important to use the PAST PERFECT when *when* means *before* in order to avoid confusion.

Charlie *had packed* his lunch *when* Sam picked him up.

However, we use only the PAST PERFECT when *before* is the last word in the clause or sentence.

Sam *had* never *used* the camera before. (= before that time)

4. We often use the PAST PERFECT with these words:

just
recently
already
scarcely
barely
ever
never
yet
still

(These adverbs usually come between *had* and the *past participle*.)

He *had* just *fed* his sandwich to some animals.

He *had* never *seen* a lion so close before.

Instead of meaning ''before now'' as they do with the PRESENT PERFECT, these words mean ''before *then*'' with the PAST PERFECT.

We also use the PAST PERFECT with *since* and *for* if we know when an activity began before another past activity, or how long it went on.

I realized that I *hadn't eaten* a single French fry since I started my diet.

Note that the PAST PERFECT is not an independent tense. It is used with the PAST TENSE in either the sentence or context.

5.	We often use the PAST PERFECT in noun clauses—frequently when we use indirect speech. "I found the trail," he said. = He said he *had found* the trail. "I've found the trail," he said. = He said he *had found* the trail.	
6.		When the main verb of a sentence is in the PAST PERFECT and the action in a relative clause occurs at the *same time*, we use the SIMPLE PAST for the verb in the relative clause. The animals had been in cages that *looked* like jail cells. NOTE: For a complete chart of tenses in relative clauses, see page 158 in the Appendix.

FILL IT IN

DIRECTIONS: Fill in the blanks in the following story with the SIMPLE PAST or PAST PERFECT tense. Remember that more than one tense may be possible in some of the blanks.

AN OUTING

Sam and Charlie (1)_____ (go) to Lion Country Safari last weekend. They

(2)_____ (never be) there before, so they (3)_____ (be) really

excited.

They (4)_____ (go) to a small zoo a few months before. There, the animals

(5)_____ (be) in cages that (6)_____ (look) like jail cells, and they

(7)_____ (sleep) on cold, cement floors. They (8)_____ (look)

miserable.

But at Lion Country Safari, the animals (9)_____ (be) almost as free to roam

as they (10)_____ (be) back in Africa. They (11)_____ (eat),

(12)_____ (sleep), (13)_____ (fight), and (14)_____

(play) just as they (15)_____ (do) in Africa—in a natural environment of dirt, trees, plants, rocks, and streams.

Sam and Charlie (16)_____ (drive) slowly through the area. At one point, a camel (17)_____ (stick) his head through the car window, and Charlie, overjoyed, (18)_____ (give) him his peanut butter sandwich. Sam (19)_____ (tell) him not to do it again because feeding the animals (20)_____ (be) against regulations. A few minutes later, they (21)_____ (be) terrified when the lions (22)_____ (come) right over to the car to "visit." Sam almost (23)_____ (drive) off the road because he (24)_____ (never see) a lion so close before. Charlie (25)_____ (not get) to see the elephants because he (26)_____ (dive) onto the floor of the car in fright at the first sight of the lions.

That afternoon, on the way home, Sam (27)_____ (be) angry with himself because he (28)_____ (forget) to bring his camera, and Charlie (29)_____ (be) hungry because he (30)_____ (feed) his lunch to the camel. But, aside from that, it (31)_____ (be) a good day.

RAP IT UP

DIRECTIONS: **A.** In the column on the left are some things that have happened to Charlie. In the column on the right are the reasons for these occurrences. Make logical sentences by combining an item from the first column with one from the second. Make as many sentences as possible in the SIMPLE PAST and the PAST PERFECT.

Example: Charlie lost weight because he had exercised.

Column 1	Column 2
not have money to pay for groceries	eat too much
pass his English test	go to bed late
take the bus to work	not read directions
lose weight	go on a diet
get a promotion	lose his wallet
borrow money from Sam	forget to set his alarm
wake up late	spend all his money on candy
become overweight	exercise
ruin a cake	work hard
fail his French test	not understand the lesson
get tired	someone—steal car
be late for work	study very hard

B. Work with a partner. Using the following schedule of Sam's life, ask and answer as many logical questions as possible. Use the SIMPLE PAST and the PAST PERFECT. The question words at right will help you get started.

Examples: —Where had he worked before he returned to medical school?
—He'd worked in a restaurant.
—How many restaurants had he worked in?
—He'd worked in three.

Sam

	15 years ago	5 years ago	last year	question words
education	finish 3rd year at Lawson Med. School drop out of Lawson	go back to Lawson	graduate from Lawson	How long ago How many times How many years Where When
career	work in restaurant after leaving school	quit 3rd restaurant in 10 years	begin work at hospital	
travel	week's vacation in Boston	2 weeks in Boston	move to Boston	
love life	break up with 5th girlfriend in one year meet Mary Lou in Boston	propose to Mary Lou in Boston	marry Mary Lou	

C. Make your own schedule for education, career, and so on, like the one above. Exchange schedules with your neighbor and ask each other questions using the SIMPLE PAST and the PAST PERFECT. You may ask questions that bring in information not on the schedule.

DIRECTIONS: Read the story on the left. When you finish, go back to the beginning, cover up the story to the left, and choose the correct tense for each capitalized simple form of the verb to the right of the picture.

THE
SPY

—I think we should give Agent Dudley Dangerfield his old job back. He has a lot of experience. He *had been spying* for the Zenrovian government since 1975 when he *decided* to come to us.

He *had been doing* a good job for us until he *went* over to "the other side."

The queen of Zenrovia *gave* him a large sum of money when he *left*.

—I don't know, Chief. I *heard* some bad things about him while I *was checking* his employment record.

—I think we should give Agent Dudley Dangerfield his old job back. He has a lot of experience. He SPY for the Zenrovian government since 1975 when he DECIDE to come to us.

He DO a good job for us until he GO over to "the other side."

The queen of Zenrovia GIVE him a large sum of money when he LEAVE.

—I don't know, Chief. I HEAR some bad things about him while I CHECK his employment record.

I *found out* that the queen *was* only *trying* to make him leave quickly because he *had been making* so many mistakes.

I FIND OUT that the queen only TRY to make him leave quickly because he MAKE so many mistakes.

For example, he *took* secret photographs of the wrong military installation although he *had been studying* the maps for three months.

For example, he TAKE secret photographs of the wrong military installation although he STUDY the maps for three months.

Then, while he *was taking* the photographs, he almost *fell* out of the plane.

Then, while he TAKE the photographs, he almost FALL out of the plane.

—That was probably because he *had been taking* flying lessons only since February.

—That was probably because he TAKE flying lessons only since February.

—Of course, there *was* also the problem with the ambassador.

—Of course, there BE also the problem with the ambassador.

Dangerfield *had been guarding* him for about a week when the ambassador *went* for a walk in the park.

Dangerfield GUARD him for about a week when the ambassador GO for a walk in the park.

While Dangerfield *was flirting* with a girl in the park, three men *kidnapped* the ambassador.

The kidnapping *caused* problems for Dangerfield, because he *had been hoping* for a salary increase.

Then, as you know, he *came* to work for us.

—But why *did* we *hire* such an idiot?

—Well, actually, when we hired him, we *weren't* aware of how badly he *had been doing* in Zenrovia.

And he *was doing* surprisingly well for us until the other side *offered* him more money, a yearly ocean cruise, and a home computer.

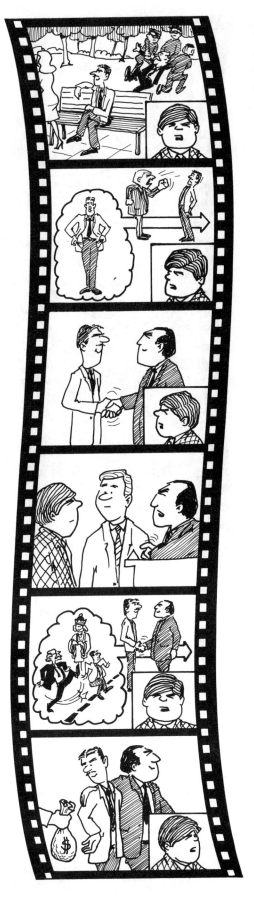

While Dangerfield FLIRT with a girl in the park, three men KIDNAP the ambassador.

The kidnapping CAUSE problems for Dangerfield, because he HOPE for a salary increase.

Then, as you know, he COME to work for us.

—But why we HIRE such an idiot?

—Well, actually, when we hired him, we NOT BE aware of how badly he DO in Zenrovia.

And he DO surprisingly well for us until the other side OFFER him more money, a yearly ocean cruise, and a home computer.

He *took* their offer and *moved* there because we *had*n't *been paying* him so well.

But he *got* into trouble last month with his boss. He *was daydreaming* one day as he *was driving* his boss to the airport. . .

. . .and he *ran into* an oak tree. His boss *flew* out of the car and *landed* in a fountain.

When they *fished* him out of the fountain, he *was yelling* something about punching Dudley Dangerfield from there to the middle of the Atlantic.

—I *was thinking* about hiring him back, but I've just changed my mind. It's good to have him on the other side.

THE END

He TAKE their offer and MOVE there because we not PAY him so well.

But he GET into trouble last month with his boss. He DAYDREAM one day as he DRIVE his boss to the airport. . .

. . .and he RUN INTO an oak tree. His boss FLY out of the car and LAND in a fountain.

When they FISH him out of the fountain, he YELL something about punching Dudley Dangerfield from there to the middle of the Atlantic.

—I THINK about hiring him back, but I've just changed my mind. It's good to have him on the other side.

PAST PERFECT CONTINUOUS	PAST CONTINUOUS
1. The PAST PERFECT CONTINUOUS is used for the duration of a single action before another action in the past. It was stopped or interrupted by the second action.  He *had been doing* a good job for us until he went over to "the other side." (He stopped doing a good job for us.) Note that the PAST PERFECT CONTINUOUS is not an independent tense. It is used with the PAST TENSE in either the sentence or context.	Sometimes people use the PAST CONTINUOUS instead of the PAST PERFECT CONTINUOUS, but it isn't quite as precise. The PAST CONTINUOUS often continues in time after the SIMPLE PAST action, but the PAST PERFECT CONTINUOUS usually stops with the second action.  He *was doing* a good job for us when "the other side" offered him a job. (Perhaps he stopped—or perhaps he continued—doing a good job for us.)
2. The PAST PERFECT CONTINUOUS can also indicate the repetition of an action before another time in the past.  He took their offer because we *hadn't been paying* him so well. (each week)	Here, too, the PAST CONTINUOUS is often used instead of the PAST PERFECT CONTINUOUS, especially if the action continues on beyond the SIMPLE PAST.  He took their offer because we *weren't paying* him very well.
3. We use the PAST PERFECT CONTINUOUS (for either reason 1 or reason 2) when we know the length of the action or when the action began. We use *for* or *since*. He *had been taking* flying lessons since February. (when he almost fell out of the plane) 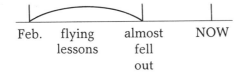	We do not use the PAST CONTINUOUS with *since* and seldom with *for*.

4.	The PAST PERFECT CONTINUOUS is not used with a specific amount or a specific number of times. For example, we do not use the PAST PERFECT CONTINUOUS with such phrases as *twice, five times, 20 pounds,* or *15 thousand dollars.* Instead, we use the PAST PERFECT with such phrases. He said he *had been losing* a lot of weight. He said he *had lost* 20 pounds.	
5.	We use the PAST PERFECT CONTINUOUS in indirect speech when the direct quote was in the PAST CONTINUOUS. "They weren't paying him very well," she said. = She said they *hadn't been paying* him very well.	

As with the other continuous tenses, we do not use either the PAST PERFECT CONTINUOUS or the PAST CONTINUOUS with NON-ACTION verbs. (See the Appendix, page 155.)

To check the use of the SIMPLE PAST, refer to chapters 5, 6, 7, and 9.

PICTURE PUZZLE

DIRECTIONS: On another piece of paper, write out the following story. Change all of the pictures and symbols to words. The character is Dudley Dangerfield (from the story earlier in this chapter), but you should use pronouns whenever possible. For each of the encircled verbs, choose the SIMPLE PAST, PAST CONTINUOUS, or PAST PERFECT CONTINUOUS.

One day a few years ago, Dudley decided to take a vacation from spying. But . . .

A DAY IN THE LIFE OF DUDLEY DANGERFIELD

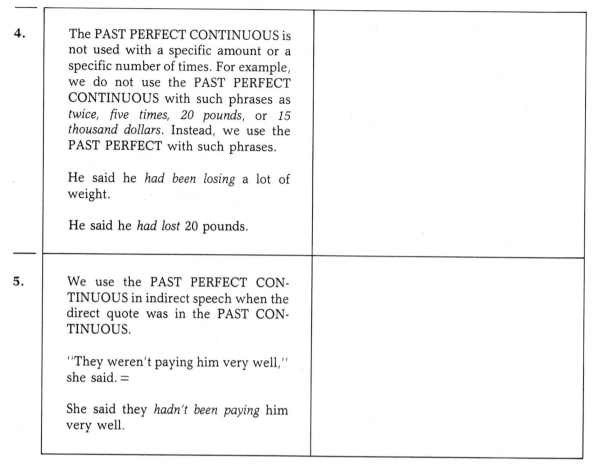

(GET) HIS 1ST JOB AS A SPY. [icon] (DECIDE) → GO [icon] A DIET, SWEAT [X] THE SAUNA EVERY [sun icon], & JOG 5 MILES EVERY [A.M.]. [icon] (THINK) ABOUT GETTING [X] SHAPE FOR THE ANNUAL INTERNATIONAL SPY [racket icon] TOURNAMENT WHEN SUDDENLY [icon] (HEAR) A LOUD SCREAM FROM SOMEWHERE ↓ THE [beach icon].

[icon] (JUMP) ↑ & (RUN) ↓ THE [beach icon] → SEE WHAT THE COMMOTION (BE). [icon] (SEE) A WOMAN [X] THE [water icon]. SHE (SCREAM) & (THRASH) [arrow] & (APPEAR) → BE DROWNING. [icon] THE [beach icon], A FEW [people icon] (RUN) [arrow] & (TRY) → FIND A LIFEGUARD. [icon] (JUMP) [X], (SWIM) [arrow], & (PULL) HER → SHORE. SOMEONE [icon] THE [beach icon] (SPREAD) A [towel icon] [icon] THE SAND, & [icon] (PUT) HER [icon] IT. SOMEONE ELSE [X] THE CROWD (SAY) THAT THE WOMAN (TRY) → SWIM → SHORE FROM A [boat icon]. FINALLY, THE WOMAN (OPEN) HER [eyes icon], & [icon] (SEE) THAT SHE (BE) FINE. [icon] ALSO (NOTICE) THAT SHE (BE) GORGEOUS. [icon] (QUICKLY FALL) [X] LOVE W/ HER WHEN THE POLICE (RUN) ↑ & (ARREST) HER. THEY (SAY) THAT SHE (BE) AN INTERNATIONAL CRIMINAL WHO (FOLLOW) [icon] FOR SEVERAL WEEKS. SHE (PLAN) → KIDNAP [icon] FOR HER GOVERNMENT SINCE THE 1ST OF THE MONTH. THE POLICE (TRY) → CAPTURE HER SINCE SHE (GET) → HAWAII.

THAT [P.M.], WHILE THE [sun icon] (SLOWLY SET), [icon] (TAKE) A WALK ↑ THE [beach icon]. AS [icon] (WALK), [icon] (THINK) W/ REGRET ABOUT HIS WOULD-BE ROMANCE. [icon] (CONSIDER) EXPLORING A NEW LINE OF WORK.

RAP IT UP

DIRECTIONS: **A.** Look at the following columns and ask a partner questions using the PAST CONTINUOUS or PAST PERFECT CONTINUOUS tense and a phrase from Column 1. To answer, your partner will use as many phrases from Column 2 as possible.

Examples:
—What had Dudley been doing when the car crashed?
—He had been driving all night when the car crashed.
—What was Dudley doing when the phone rang?
—He was smoking a cigarette when the phone rang.

Column 1	Column 2
fire break out	mow the lawn all afternoon
train crash	smoke a cigarette
storm start	study maps for 3 hours
earthquake occur	drive a car all night
phone ring	feed the cat
lights go out	learn to fly for 4 weeks
tires blow out	wind up a toy
dog bite	operate a computer
bee sting	chase a spy

B. Ask your partner questions about his/her day using HOW LONG and the PAST PERFECT CONTINUOUS tense. Here is a suggestion:

Example:
—How long had you been sitting in class when the bell rang?
—I'd been sitting there for 20 minutes when the bell rang.

bell ring	fall asleep	alarm go off
teacher walk into class	lesson begin	bus arrive

11 PAST TENSE REVIEW

DIRECTIONS: Fill in the blanks with the following tenses. In some cases, more than one tense is possible.

SIMPLE PAST
PAST CONTINUOUS
PAST PERFECT
PAST PERFECT CONTINUOUS

HOW I CHANGED MY LIFE

I go to the Gorgeous Body Health Club four times a week. When I (1)_____ (begin) going there, I (2)_____ (be) in terrible shape. I (3)_____ (not ever go) to a health club before, and I (4)_____ (not eat) right for years. On the day I (5)_____ (join) the club, I (6)_____ (be) thirty pounds overweight, and my girlfriend (7)_____ (worry) about my health for a long time.

On the first day of my new exercise program, I (8)_____ (run) a mile, (9)_____ (swim) twenty laps, (10)_____ (take) a half-hour exercise class, and (11)_____ (sweat) in the sauna. I (12)_____ (think) I was going to die! While I (13)_____ (sweat) in the sauna, I (14)_____ (dream) about going home to an enormous sandwich, French fries, a Coke, and a huge hot fudge sundae!

But at that time, nobody (15)_____ (tell) me about the diet program at the health club. I (16)_____ (change) clothes in the locker room and (17)_____ (think) about my hot fudge sundae when my exercise instructor (18)_____ (come) up and (19)_____ (tell) me that the diet class (20)_____ (just begin) and that I (21)_____ (be) five minutes late. "Diet class?" I (22)_____ (say), horrified. I (23)_____ (tell) him that nobody (24)_____ (mention) such a thing to me.

Well, I somewhat reluctantly (25)_____ (go) over to the diet class. When I (26)_____ (walk) in, a terribly thin young woman (27)_____ (give) a lecture on all the foods we shouldn't eat. She (28)_____ (point) to a list of forbidden foods which she (29)_____ (put) on the blackboard. All my hopes (30)_____ (sink) when I (31)_____ (see) all my favorite foods on the list. Then the young woman (32)_____ (say) that she (33)_____ (come) to Gorgeous Body for two years and (34)_____ (teach) the diet class for six months. She (35)_____ (tell) us she (36)_____ (weigh) 197 pounds when she (37)_____ (start) the program. Of course that (38)_____ (be) very inspiring! Everyone in the class (39)_____ (swear) to come to class regularly and to keep the strict diet.

This (40)_____ (be) all a year ago. One day at lunchtime last week, as I (41)_____ (eat) my spinach salad, I (42)_____ (think) about how my life (43)_____ (change) and how wonderful I (44)_____ (become). I (45)_____ (not eat) a single French fry since I started my diet. I (46)_____ (exercise) two hours a day for the past year. And for several weeks I (47)_____ (think) of entering the Mr. America Contest. I (48)_____ (try) many times to persuade my girlfriend to join the health club and become as healthy and as perfect as I was. However, as I (49)_____ (drink) my nonfat milk, I sadly (50)_____ (remember) that she (51)_____ (recently leave) me. She said that I (52)_____ (become) a new person but that she (53)_____ (prefer) the old me to the thin, vain one. She said it seemed that I (54)_____ (trade in) a pleasant personality for a Mr. America body, and she didn't think it was a good trade.

DIRECTIONS: Use the phrases and pictures on this page to help you rewrite Harry's story. DO NOT LOOK BACK AT THE ORIGINAL STORY. Your story won't be exactly the same as the original, but you should correctly use the four tenses from this unit. The verbs on this page are in either picture form or the simple form, but you will choose from the following tenses when you rewrite the story on the next page: SIMPLE PAST, PAST CONTINUOUS, PAST PERFECT, and PAST PERFECT CONTINUOUS. Instead of telling the story in the first person (I/my/we), use the third person (he/his/them).

CUE SHEET

1. never go before
   not eat right
   girlfriend

2.

3. nobody tell
   change clothes
   come up
   "The diet class has just begun."
   nobody mention

4. "I've been coming here for 2 years, and I've been teaching this class for 6 months. I weighed 197 pounds two years ago."

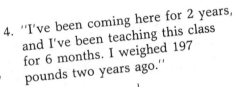

5. not eat a single French fry
   exercise 2 hours a day for a year
   think of entering Mr. America
   Contest
   girlfriend recently leave
   "You have become a new person, but I loved the old one."

HOW HARRY CHANGED HIS LIFE

When Harry began going to the Gorgeous Body Health Club, he had never gone to a health club before, and he ...

DIRECTIONS: **A.** Use the following Story Line to help you answer the questions on the next page. This Story Line will help you understand how Harry (the fellow at the Gorgeous Body Health Club) came to be overweight in the first place. The verbs on this page are all in the simple form. You should choose the correct tense.

HARRY'S LIFE

1955	1959	1960	1961
BE BORN IN NEW YORK CITY	BEGIN NURSERY SCHOOL	BEGIN KINDERGARTEN	(FAMILY) MOVE TO THE SUBURBS
LIVE ON 23RD FLOOR OF A SKYSCRAPER	(A LITTLE KID) HIT HIM, (NOSE) BLEED, CLING TO TEACHER	BE VERY SHY WANT A DOG	GET A DOG START FIRST GRADE BE VERY SHY

1962	1964	1965	1967	1969
FEED DOG/(DOG) BITE HARRY	RIDE FIRST HORSE	FALL OFF HORSE & BREAK ARM	GO CAMPING WITH PARENTS	GO HUNTING/ SHOOT HIMSELF IN THE FOOT BY ACCIDENT
BEGIN TO BE AFRAID OF DOGS	BEGIN HORSEBACK RIDING LESSONS	BEGIN TO BE AFRAID OF HORSES	SLEEP OUTDOORS FOR THE FIRST TIME	BE IN THE HOSPITAL FOR A WEEK
GIVE DOG AWAY	FIGHT WITH A KID, GET A BLACK EYE	QUIT RIDING	SWIM IN LAKE/ ALMOST DROWN	BEGIN TO BE AFRAID OF GUNS, HUNTING, & HOSPITALS
			BEGIN TO BE SCARED OF SWIMMING	

1970	1973	1975	1977	1978
TAKE FIRST DANCING LESSON/ STEP ON HIS PARTNER'S FOOT	CONTINUE EATING TOO MUCH	BE OVERWEIGHT	CONTINUE TO EAT & BE OVERWEIGHT	CONTINUE TO BE OVERWEIGHT
(SHE) TEASE HIM	START COLLEGE IN FALL	DRIVE TO STORE/ DAYDREAM ABOUT BECOMING A ROCK STAR/ GET IN AN ACCIDENT	GRADUATE FROM COLLEGE	CONTINUE TO LOOK FOR A JOB
BEGIN TO BE SHY WITH GIRLS	MOVE TO CAMPUS	CHANGE MAJOR FROM MUSIC TO COMPUTER SCIENCE	LOOK FOR A JOB (JUNE-DEC.)	
BEGIN TO EAT TOO MUCH	STUDY MUSIC			

1979	1982	The year before last	Last year
FIND A JOB AS A COMPUTER PROGRAMMER	FIND A GIRLFRIEND	JOIN "GORGEOUS BODY HEALTH CLUB" (DEC.)	CONTINUE GOING TO THE CLUB, LOSE 30 LBS. & ALL HIS SHYNESS
CONTINUE TO BE OVERWEIGHT		BEGIN TO JOG, SWIM, TAKE EXERCISE CLASSES, DIET	GET A DOG; GO CAMPING; BEGIN HORSEBACK RIDING
			BECOME SELFISH, SUPERFICIAL, & OVERLY CONFIDENT
			(GIRLFRIEND) LEAVE HIM
			QUIT HEALTH CLUB
			(GIRLFRIEND) COME BACK

B. Look at the Story Line on the previous page and answer these questions. Use the following tenses: SIMPLE PAST, PAST CONTINUOUS, PAST PERFECT, and PAST PERFECT CONTINUOUS.

1. Where was Harry's family living when he was born?
2. When did he begin nursery school?
3. What happened one day at nursery school? What else? Who did he cling to?
4. When he began kindergarten in 1960, had he been to school before?
5. Where did the family move in 1961? What did they get?
6. How long had Harry been having problems with shyness when he started the first grade?
7. Why did Harry begin to be afraid of dogs? What was he doing when this happened? What did they do with the dog?
8. When did he ride his first horse? Where was the family living when he began riding lessons?
9. What happened one day in 1964?
10. How long had he been taking riding lessons when he decided to quit? Why did he decide to quit?
11. What happened when he went camping with his parents?
12. Why was he in the hospital for a week? What was he doing when this happened?
13. Why did his dance partner tease him at his first lesson?
14. Why do you think he began to eat too much?
15. What was he doing in December, 1973? How many homes had he had when he moved to campus?
16. What was he doing while he was driving to the store one day in 1975? What happened?
17. How long had he been studying computer science when he graduated?
18. What was he doing in October, 1977?
19. How long had he been looking for a job when he found the job as a computer programmer?
20. What changed his life the year before last? Why was Harry overweight at the time he joined the club?
21. Why do you think he became more confident? How did he overcome his fears and his shyness?
22. Why did his girlfriend leave him? Why did she come back?

IT'S YOUR TURN: Have a "THERAPY SESSION." In a group of 3-4 students, one student will make a statement about himself. (*Examples:* I'm shy./I'm afraid of water./I hate cats./I'm an engineer.) The other students will ask questions to find out the steps that led to this fear/job/condition. Use the PAST, PAST CONTINUOUS, PAST PERFECT, and PAST PERFECT CONTINUOUS.

Examples: —I hate cats.
                    —When did you first notice this?
                    —Well, a cat bit me when I was 12.
                    —Had you been around cats before that time?

Then a second student will make a statement and answer questions, and so on.

DIRECTIONS: Fill in the blanks with the tenses we've studied so far. In some cases, more than one tense may be possible.

SIMPLE PRESENT   PAST CONTINUOUS
PRESENT CONTINUOUS   FUTURE IN THE PAST (*was/were going to* or *would*)
PRESENT PERFECT   PAST PERFECT
PRESENT PERFECT CONTINUOUS   PAST PERFECT CONTINUOUS
SIMPLE PAST

MY TWO CAREERS

I.

One summer when I (1)_____ (be) a teenager, I (2)_____ (get) a job with a circus. As part of my job, I

(3)_____ (stick) up posters all over the city,

(4)_____ (set) up chairs in the tent, and

(5)_____ (sell) tickets. I (6)_____

(learn) a lot about circus life that summer, and I

(7)_____ (love) circuses ever since then.

Unfortunately, the circus that I (8)_____ (work) for

(9)_____ (not be) a very successful one. Things

(10)_____ (forever go) wrong. One night, for example, we

(11)_____ (begin) the performance very late. I (12)_____ (already

shut) down the box office, and everyone (13)_____ (sit) in the tent. The audience

(14)_____ (already eat) all of the hot dogs and ice cream cones, and they

(15)_____ (grow) restless. I (16)_____ (think) that the crowd

(17)_____ (throw) tomatoes or something at the ringmaster because they

(18)_____ (be) so irritated. Finally, the show (19)_____ (begin).

The ringmaster (20)_____ (lead) the parade of animals and performers into

the tent. He (21)_____ (look) quite nervous because the gypsy

fortune-teller who always (22)_____ (travel)

with the circus (23)_____ (see) terrible things

in her crystal ball all day long. She (24)_____

(warn) him for weeks not to put on this performance, and he

(25)_____ (threaten) to fire her unless she

(26)_____ (give) him some better predictions.

Anyway, I (27)_____ (watch) the whole show that night. Everything
(28)_____ (go) fine at first. Three elephants (29)_____ (do) tricks in
the center ring. In another ring, the lion tamer (30)_____ (get) one of his lions to
jump through a ring of fire. The lion (31)_____ (be) very cranky all day, but she
(32)_____ (do) pretty well that night. In the other ring, twelve clowns (33)_____
(try) to stuff themselves into a small car while the stunt coordinator (34)_____ (yell)
directions at them. At the same time, above the center ring,
two tightrope walkers (35)_____ (already climb)
their ladders and (36)_____ (just step) out onto
the tightrope.

II.

Then it (37)_____ (happen). One of the tightrope
walkers, who (38)_____ (catch) a cold a few days before,
suddenly (39)_____ (sneeze). He (40)_____
(lose) his balance and (41)_____ (crash) into the safety
net. His partner (42)_____ (look) down for just a second,
and then he (43)_____ (lose) his balance, too. He
(44)_____ (catch) the tightrope with his right hand as he
(45)_____ (fall), and he (46)_____ (hang) there
for several seconds, trying to figure out what to do next. He
(47)_____ (sweat) with fear because he
(48)_____ (see) that the safety net (49)_____
(collapse) just after his partner (50)_____ (fall) into it. The
audience, horrified, (51)_____ (hold) its breath.

The tightrope walker (52)_____ (cling) to the rope for as
long as possible, and then he (53)_____ (let) go. I (54)_____ (be) sure
that I (55)_____ (faint). The whole audience (56)_____ (know) that the
poor guy (57)_____ (probably break) his neck in the fall.

However, instead of crashing to his death, he (58)_____ (fall) onto one of the
elephants, (59)_____ (slide) off the elephant's back, and (60)_____
(land) softly on the floor of the tent. He (61)_____ (be) fine, but the elephant,
shocked by this unexpected creature on her back, (62)_____ (flee) to the next ring,
where the clowns (63)_____ (just squeeze) into the car and (64)_____
(now try) to wiggle out. The elephant (65)_____ (run)
past the clowns toward the ringmaster, who (66)_____
(split) his pants while he (67)_____ (try) to climb over

a low wall to get away. Then the elephant (68)_____ (head) for the ring with the
lions, where the lion tamer (69)_____ (run) back and forth, trying to capture his
lions and put them back in their cages. I (70)_____ (wonder) what (71)_____
(happen) next when the lions, nervous and confused, (72)_____ (spring) out of the
ring, into the audience. Terrified people (73)_____ (flee) in all directions. Others
(74)_____ (hide) under their seats. Nobody (75)_____ (be) hurt, but
several days later, the owners of the circus (76)_____ (choose) to go out of
business because this kind of thing (77)_____ (forever happen).

III.

My short career with the circus (78)_____ (begin) and (79)_____
(end) over two decades ago. I (80)_____ (wait on) tables for a few years after
finishing high school, and then I (81)_____ (go) to college. I (82)_____
(work) in a bank ever since I (83)_____ (graduate) from college. It
(84)_____ (be) a very boring line of work. I
(85)_____ (sit) at a desk all day and seldom
(86)_____ (have) an opportunity to meet any interesting
people. I (87)_____ (answer) questions and
(88)_____ (give) financial advice whenever anyone
(89)_____ (come) in and (90)_____ (ask) for a loan. Last year, one of
the bank tellers (91)_____ (steal) $20,000 from the bank, and this year, three
people (92)_____ (try) to rob the bank, but aside from that, nothing exciting ever
(93)_____ (happen). Right now, for example, I (94)_____ (sit) at my
desk and (95)_____ (hope) that the phone won't ring. I (96)_____
(daydream) about doing something exciting: going on a safari through the jungle, taking a
spaceship into outer space, or doing scientific experiments in a laboratory. You see, I
(97)_____ (begin) to get very restless. I (98)_____ (wear) a business
suit every business day for the past twenty years. I (99)_____ (answer) the same
questions thousands of times. I (100)_____ (not do)
anything exciting since I was a teenager. A good salary
(101)_____ (not be) enough. I (102)_____
(see) circus posters all over town this week, and I
(103)_____ (already decide) to put in my application
and trade in my business suit for a clown suit!

TELLING ABOUT AN EVENT: In a group of three students, describe the following events. Each student should take a different point of view of the same event. Tell the other students 1) where you were, 2) what you saw, 3) how you felt, 4) what you were doing at the time, 5) what you thought was going to happen, 6) what you did, 7) how this has changed your life, and 8) what you've been doing since then. Use your imagination!

1. A CIRCUS PERFORMANCE

Student A	Student B	Student C
You were in the audience at the performance.	You were the ringmaster of the circus.	You were a tight-rope walker in the performance.

2. A BANK ROBBERY

Student A	Student B	Student C
You were a customer standing in line at the bank.	You were a bank teller.	You were the bank robber.

3. A SIMILAR SITUATION OF YOUR OWN

INTERVIEW: With one other student, role-play a job interview. Use all of the tenses we've studied so far.

1. AT A CIRCUS

Student A	Student B
You are a circus owner/manager.	You want a job as a clown OR a tightrope walker OR a lion tamer.

2. AT A BANK

Student A	Student B
You are a bank manager.	You want a job as a teller OR a loan officer OR a security guard.

3. ANOTHER JOB INTERVIEW OF YOUR CHOICE

Example: —What kind of work are you doing now?
—Well, I'm unemployed at the moment.
—Have you worked as a _____ before?
—Yes, I've had a lot of experience.

And so on.

FUTURE

SIMPLE FUTURE: WILL/BE GOING TO

DIRECTIONS: Read the following story. When you finish, go back to the beginning, cover up the story to the left, and choose the correct tense for each capitalized simple form of the verb to the right of the picture.

—Good evening, ladies and gentlemen. Tonight you*'re going to hear* what the candidates have to say.

—Good evening, ladies and gentlemen. Tonight you HEAR what the candidates have to say.

We have with us Mrs. Laura Kent and her husband, Brad, and Mr. Eugene Talamany and his wife, Myra. Mrs. Kent, *will* you *begin*, please?

We have with us Mrs. Laura Kent and her husband, Brad, and Mr. Eugene Talamany and his wife, Myra. Mrs. Kent, you BEGIN, please?

—Thank you. Ladies and gentlemen, you*'re going to make* a very important decision next Tuesday. The choice *will be* yours.

—Thank you. Ladies and gentlemen, you MAKE a very important decision next Tuesday. The choice BE yours.

If you elect me, I *will work* for the good of everyone while Mr. Talamany *will work* for a select few.

If you elect me, I WORK for the good of everyone while Mr. Talamany WORK for a select few.

I *will spend* your money carefully. My experience with the family budget has taught me to be economical.

Mr. Talamany, on the other hand, *is going to be* quite generous with your money. He'*ll spend* it mostly on big lunches and expensive vacations.

However, if you elect me, I *will see* to it that we build more schools. With our current population growth, we'*re going to need* more classrooms in the near future.

Mr. Talamany *will* perhaps *promise* more jobs and money for the needy. But promises are all that you *will get*.

Your money *will disappear*, and, until the next election, so *will* Mr. Talamany.

Mr. Talamany says he *will attend* all important meetings. But, as we've seen in the past, he'*ll sleep* through them all.

I SPEND your money carefully. My experience with the family budget has taught me to be economical.

Mr. Talamany, on the other hand, BE quite generous with your money. He SPEND it mostly on big lunches and expensive vacations.

However, if you elect me, I SEE to it that we build more schools. With our current population growth, we NEED more classrooms in the near future.

Mr. Talamany perhaps PROMISE more jobs and money for the needy. But promises are all that you GET.

Your money DISAPPEAR and, until the next election, so (—) Mr. Talamany.

Mr. Talamany says he ATTEND all important meetings. But, as we've seen in the past, he SLEEP through them all.

Are you *going to let* this happen or *are* you *going to vote* for me next Tuesday?

You LET this happen or you VOTE for me next Tuesday?

—Thank you, Mrs. Kent. Mr. Talamany, *will* you *respond*, please?

—Thank you, Mrs. Kent. Mr. Talamany, you RESPOND, please?

—Thank you, ladies and gentlemen. I'*m going to tell* you why I'm the best candidate for the job.

—Thank you, ladies and gentlemen. I TELL you why I'm the best candidate for the job.

You need a man for this job, and I *will be* that man.

You need a man for this job, and I BE that man.

A woman's place is in the kitchen. After the election, we'*re going to send* Mrs. Kent back home to be a good wife like my little woman, Myra, here.

A woman's place is in the kitchen. After the election, we SEND Mrs. Kent back home to be a good wife like my little woman, Myra, here.

Mrs. Kent says we'*re going to need* more schools. We don't need more schools. *Shall* I *tell* you what we're really *going to need*? We'*re going to need* new offices for our elected officials.

Mrs. Kent says we NEED more schools. We don't need more schools. I TELL you what we really NEED? We NEED new offices for our elected officials.

Contrary to what Mrs. Kent says, I *will lower* unemployment in our city. The city *will hire* as many able-bodied men as possible.

We already have too many women taking jobs away from men. If you elect Mrs. Kent, you*'ll make* the problem worse.

I*'m not going to stand by* and *watch* a woman ruin our city!

—Excuse me. Goodbye, Eugene. I *won't be* your ''little woman'' anymore. I*'m going to vote* for Mrs. Kent next Tuesday.

—But, Myra, sweetheart, if you leave, who*'s going to take* care of me?

THE END

Contrary to what Mrs. Kent says, I LOWER unemployment in our city. The city HIRE as many able-bodied men as possible.

We already have too many women taking jobs away from men. If you elect Mrs. Kent, you MAKE the problem worse.

I NOT STAND BY and WATCH a woman ruin our city!

—Excuse me. Goodbye, Eugene. I NOT BE your ''little woman'' anymore. I VOTE for Mrs. Kent next Tuesday.

—But, Myra, sweetheart, if you leave, who TAKE care of me?

FUTURE: WILL + SIMPLE FORM	FUTURE: BE GOING TO + SIMPLE FORM

```
                    |_____×
                   NOW         FUTURE
```

1.	WILL (+ SIMPLE FORM) indicates *promise*, *determination*, *volunteered action*, *prediction*, or *inevitability* for the future. Your money *will disappear*. (prediction) We'*ll need* more schools. (inevitability) I'*ll spend* your money carefully. (promise) This city *will hire* as many people as possible. (determination)	BE GOING TO (+ SIMPLE FORM) indicates *prediction* and *inevitability* but not usually promise, determination, or a volunteered action. = Your money *is going to disappear*. (prediction) = We'*re going to need* more schools. (inevitability)
2.	In the negative, WILL NOT (WON'T) can mean *refusal*, besides the negative of the meanings above in 1. I *won't let* this happen. (= I refuse to let this happen.)	BE GOING TO can also indicate refusal. I'*m not going to let* this happen. (= I refuse to let this happen.)
3.	We do not use WILL for an action or event planned for the future.	BE GOING TO indicates an action or event *planned* with some certainty for the future. *Are* you *going to vote* for me? I'*m going to vote* for Mrs. Kent.
4.	WILL is used in polite requests and invitations. In this usage, it is interchangeable with *would* and *could*. *Will* you *begin*, please?	We do not use BE GOING TO for requests and invitations.
5.	SHALL (another form of WILL) in American English is mainly used with *I* or *we* in the question form: *Shall* I *tell* you what we need? *Shall* we *begin*? (In statements, SHALL is considered very formal in American English.)	

FILL IT IN

DIRECTIONS: Fill in the blanks in the following story with the FUTURE tense using either "will" or "be going to." Remember that more than one tense is possible in some of the blanks.

ANOTHER POLITICAL CAMPAIGN

Lionel is running for president of his elementary school. He (1)_____ (be) in the sixth grade next year. He thinks he (2)_____ (be) very important then. Lionel promises to help all students. He says he (3)_____ (fire) all the cooks and (4)_____ (hire) new ones. His new cooks (5)_____ (fix) cheeseburgers, hot dogs, and French fries. They (6)_____ (serve) ice cream sundaes and chocolate cake for dessert every day. Lionel says that if he is elected, the school (7)_____ (have) longer recesses and shorter class sessions. He (8)_____ (cut) the school day in half. That way, he says, everyone (9)_____ (have) more time to play ball and do other important things.

Lionel (10)_____ (work) hard to win this election. He (11)_____ (give) a speech at every recess. He (12)_____ (promise) new balls and a larger play yard. He says he (13)_____ (make) the school principal provide computer games and lots of new toys for everyone. The school (14)_____ (provide) snacks for every recess.

After school today, Lionel (15)_____ (stop) off at the stationery store. He (16)_____ (buy) cardboard, crayons, and glue. Then, at home, he (17)_____ (work) on his campaign posters. He (18)_____ (draw) pictures of the school on some posters and (19)_____ (glue) photographs of himself onto others. His posters (20)_____ (say) that he (21)_____ (cut out) homework and tests. Students (22)_____ (be able) to grade themselves. The teachers (23)_____ (have to) make every class interesting, or the students (24)_____ (find) a new teacher.

Lionel (25)_____ (be) very busy on election day. He (26)_____ (give) every student who votes for him a piece of bubble gum. That way, he (27)_____ (be) sure to win.

DIRECTIONS: **A.** Laura Kent has worked hard in her campaign. Next week she's going to take a vacation. Using her calendar below, tell about her plans.

	Monday	Tuesday	Wednesday	Thursday	Friday
Morning					
Afternoon					
Evening					

B. Pretend you are running for public office. Using the following phrases and some of your own, make a campaign speech, using "will" and "be going to."

PHRASES

build more schools	put in new street lights
promote better education	send criminals to jail
clean up the city	lower taxes
provide jobs	balance the budget
help the needy	listen to the voters

C. Work with a partner. Talk about the coming week. Be sure to include plans, predictions, promises, things you're determined to do, and things that are inevitable. Use both "will" and "be going to." Listen to your partner carefully so that you may ask questions for further information.

Example: —What are you going to do next Monday?
            —I'm going to go to the doctor.
            —Why are you going to go to the doctor?
            —Because I . . .

DIRECTIONS: Read the story on the left. When you finish, go back to the beginning, cover up the story to the left, and choose the correct tense for each capitalized simple form of the verb to the right of the picture.

—So! Robert and Suzanne, you*'re going to get* married, and you want to know your future.

I*'ll look* into my crystal ball and *tell* you everything.

Your wedding *begins* at 2:00 next Saturday. But—oh dear—I see that Suzanne *will be* late.

Just before she *gets* to the church, Robert's nephew *is going to swallow* the wedding ring. You*'ll have to* use Robert's high school ring, instead.

—So! Robert and Suzanne, you GET married, and you want to know your future.

I LOOK into my crystal ball and TELL you everything.

Your wedding BEGIN at 2:00 next Saturday. But—oh dear—I see that Suzanne BE late.

Just before she GET to the church, Robert's nephew SWALLOW the wedding ring. You HAVE TO use Robert's high school ring, instead.

When the ceremony *is* over, you*'ll leave* for your honeymoon. Your plane *takes off* at 6:00.

Unfortunately, you *won't be* able to go to Hawaii because Robert *will lose* the tickets before your taxi *reaches* the airport.

Oh, dear. You*'ll spend* your honeymoon at a miserable, cold hotel downtown instead of going to Hawaii.

Suzanne *is going to catch* a terrible cold and *sneeze* for three straight days before you both *give up* and *go* home.

Tsk, tsk. As soon as you *move* into your little house, Robert, your brother *will lose* his job and *move* in with you.

He*'s going to bring* his wife, four kids, dog, and cat with him.

When the ceremony BE over, you LEAVE for your honeymoon. Your plane TAKE off at 6:00.

Unfortunately, you NOT BE ABLE to go to Hawaii because Robert LOSE the tickets before your taxi REACH the airport.

Oh, dear. You SPEND your honeymoon at a miserable, cold hotel downtown instead of going to Hawaii.

Suzanne CATCH a terrible cold and SNEEZE for three straight days before you both GIVE UP and GO home.

Tsk, tsk. As soon as you MOVE into your little house, Robert, your brother LOSE his job and MOVE in with you.

He BRING his wife, four kids, dog, and cat with him.

Unfortunately, your house *won't be* a very quiet place until he *finds* a job and *moves* out.

But, on the other hand, things *will get* better. Soon after your children *are* born, you and Robert *are going to buy* a small grocery store and *fix* it up.

You*'ll work* very hard for several years.

Unless something very unusual *happens*, your little store *will become* a success.

As soon as you *save* enough money, you*'ll buy* another store, and another, and another, and another.

You*'ll own* a chain of supermarkets by the time your kids *finish* college.

Unfortunately, your house NOT BE a very quiet place until he FIND a job and MOVE out.

But, on the other hand, things GET better. Soon after your children BE born, you and Robert BUY a small grocery store and FIX it up.

You WORK very hard for several years.

Unless something very unusual HAPPEN, your little store BECOME a success.

As soon as you SAVE enough money, you BUY another store, and another, and another, and another.

You OWN a chain of supermarkets by the time your kids FINISH college.

Soon after you *open* your fourteenth store, you*'ll move* into a big mansion.

Your daughter *will become* president of the country, and your son *is going to explore* outer space.

When you*'re* old, you*'ll sit* by the pool and *remember* the past.

You*'re going to be* rich. Your kids *are going to be* famous.

That'll be $10.00.

THE END

Soon after you OPEN your fourteenth store, you MOVE into a big mansion.

Your daughter BECOME president of the country, and your son EXPLORE outer space.

When you BE old, you SIT by the pool and REMEMBER the past.

You BE rich. Your kids BE famous.

That'll be $10.00.

SIMPLE PRESENT	SIMPLE FUTURE: WILL/BE GOING TO

On a time line, the SIMPLE PRESENT (meaning the future) looks like the other future tenses. However, it is used differently.

NOW   FUTURE

1.

The SIMPLE PRESENT has a future meaning in subordinate clauses that express *time* and *condition* with these words:

when
whenever
while
as (= while)
until } TIME
before
after
as soon as
by the time

if
unless } CONDITION
in case

Unless something unusual *happens,* your store will become a success.

As soon as you *save* enough money, you'll buy another store.

The subordinate clause may come before the main clause (see the examples above), in which case there is a comma, or it may come after the main clause, in which case there is no comma:

Your store will become a success unless something unusual *happens.*

The PRESENT PERFECT is sometimes used instead of the SIMPLE PRESENT in a clause. It emphasizes completion of the activity in the clause.

As soon as you *'ve saved* enough money, you'll buy another store.

WILL or BE GOING TO is used in the main clause of a future tense sentence that contains a subordinate clause of *time* or *condition*.

The main clause determines the tense of the whole sentence:

When the ceremony *is* over, the couple *leaves* for the honeymoon. = PRESENT (after *every* wedding)

When the ceremony *is* over, the couple *will leave* for the honeymoon. = FUTURE (after *this* wedding)

Although WILL or BE GOING TO or the PRESENT CONTINUOUS (see Chapter 15) may be used in the main clause, WILL is perhaps most commonly used, even when it expresses a *plan.*

2.

The SIMPLE PRESENT has a future meaning with certain specific verbs that indicate a scheduled event: start begin end open close arrive leave take off (meaning leave) get (to) (meaning arrive) land (meaning arrive) rise (the sun, a theater curtain) set (the sun) The wedding *begins* at 2:00 next Saturday. The plane *takes off* at 6:00.	WILL and BE GOING TO are not incorrect with these verbs, but they are less common and less natural.

PICTURE PUZZLE

DIRECTIONS: On another piece of paper, write out the following story, changing all of the pictures and symbols to words. The character's name is Esmeralda (the gypsy you met earlier in this chapter), but you should use pronouns whenever possible. For each of the encircled verbs, choose the FUTURE TENSE (WILL or BE GOING TO) or the SIMPLE PRESENT TENSE (meaning the future).

Esmeralda is looking into her crystal ball to see her own future. What does she see?

GYPSY ESMERALDA'S FUTURE

🔮 SEES THAT 🔮 (HAVE) PROBLEMS W/ 💵 ☒ THE FUTURE IF SHE ~~CHANGE~~ HER WAY OF DOING BUSINESS. 🔮 (HAVE) 3 MAIN PROBLEMS.

1ST, 👥 (BEGIN) → DRIVE ⊟→ HER LITTLE SHOP ⌂ THEIR WAY → BIG SHOPPING CENTERS. 👥 ~~SEE~~ HER ⌐FORTUNES $10⌐ ☒ THE ▭ ☒ THEIR HURRY → GET → A BIG STORE.

ANOTHER PROBLEM (BE) HER 👁 SIGHT. AS 🔮 (GET) OLDER, HER 👁 SIGHT (GET) WORSE. ☒ THE FUTURE, IT (BE) DIFFICULT FOR HER → SEE IMAGES ☒ HER 🔮.

BUT [gypsy]'S WORST PROBLEM (BE) THAT [people] (STOP) BELIEVING ☒ GYPSIES W/ [crystal ball]S BECAUSE [people] (THINK) THAT [crystal ball]S ARE OUT OF STYLE. WHEN [people] (DO) THAT, [people] (STOP) GOING → FORTUNE-TELLERS, & [gypsy]'S BUSINESS (BE) ☒ TERRIBLE TROUBLE. YOUNG [people] (B̶E̶G̶) HER FOR ADVICE [TV] ROMANCE ANYMORE. ROCK STARS (O̶F̶F̶E̶R̶) HER [money] & JEWELRY FOR ADVICE [perfume] d.[music]. DETECTIVES (A̶S̶K̶) HER FOR HELP ☒ CATCHING CRIMINALS.

AS SOON AS [gypsy] (MAKE) SOME BIG CHANGES ☒ HER BUSINESS, [gypsy] (STOP) WORRYING, & [gypsy] (H̶A̶V̶E̶) ANY MORE TROUBLE W/ ULCERS. BUT BECAUSE [gypsy] (ALWAYS BE) A STUBBORN, INDEPENDENT [woman], [gypsy] (REFUSE) → MAKE ANY CHANGES UNTIL THE [city] GOVERNMENT (DECIDE) → EVICT HER & TEAR ↓ HER [house]. WHEN THEY (DO) THAT, [gypsy] (HAVE TO) MOVE HER BUSINESS → A SHOPPING CENTER. AFTER [gypsy] (MOVE), [gypsy] (GET) SOME [money] & (BUY) ADVERTISING ☒ ALL THE LOCAL [newspaper]'S. THEN [gypsy] (THROW) [out] HER [crystal ball] & (BUY) A [computer].

AS SOON AS A CUSTOMER (SEE) HER [computer], [person] (KNOW) THAT [gypsy] IS A VERY MODERN FORTUNE-TELLER. SOON, 1,000 S OF [people] (BEGIN) → COME → HER NEW SHOP. [gypsy] (HIRE) MORE [people] & (OPEN) BRANCH OFFICES. EVERY OFFICE (HAVE) A [computer]. ☒ A FEW YEARS, [gypsy] (HAVE) A WHOLE [chain] OF OFFICES, & BUSINESS (BE) TERRIFIC!

RAP IT UP

DIRECTIONS: **A.** Pretend you are a fortune teller. Tell the fortunes of the following people by combining the words on the left of the next page with as many pictures on the next page as possible. Finish the sentence with a prediction.

Examples: If she goes on a cruise, she'll meet the man of her dreams.
He'll meet the girl of his dreams when he goes on a cruise.
Before they go on a cruise, they'll. . .

If
After
As soon as
Before
Unless
By the time
While
When
In case

B. Pretend you are a fortune-teller and tell your partner his/her fortune. Use the words on the left above in your sentences.

Example: —I see that when you. . .
—And after that what am I going to do?

15

PRESENT CONTINUOUS (meaning the future)
SIMPLE FUTURE: WILL/BE GOING TO

DIRECTIONS: Read the story on the left. When you finish, go back to the beginning, cover up the story to the left, and choose the correct tense for each capitalized simple form of the verb to the right of the picture.

THE
STUNT
MAN

—Ah! Good! You're our new stunt person! You'*ll be* pretty busy today. We'*re going to begin* in about an hour.

—Ah! Good! You're our new stunt person! You BE pretty busy today. We BEGIN in about an hour.

—Great! I'*m* really *going to enjoy* working with you experienced stunt people. What *are* we *doing* today?

—Great! I really ENJOY working with you experienced stunt people. What we DO today?

—Well, you'*ll be* on top of that building and I'*ll be* down here.

—Well, you BE on top of that building and I BE down here.

You'*re going to fight* with that guy over there, and he'*ll punch* you in the face.

You FIGHT with that guy over there, and he PUNCH you in the face.

You're *going to fall* off the building. Remember that you'*ll need* to look scared while you'*re falling.*

—Oh, I'*ll remember.*

—After that, we'*re having* a car crash. You'*re going to drive* this car off that cliff into the lake.

—Which car *are* you *driving*?

—I'm not driving a car. I'm the stunt coordinator. Whenever you'*re doing* a stunt, I'*ll have* to watch and take notes. Now, let me explain this.

Be sure not to lose control of the car until you'*re going* 80 miles per hour.

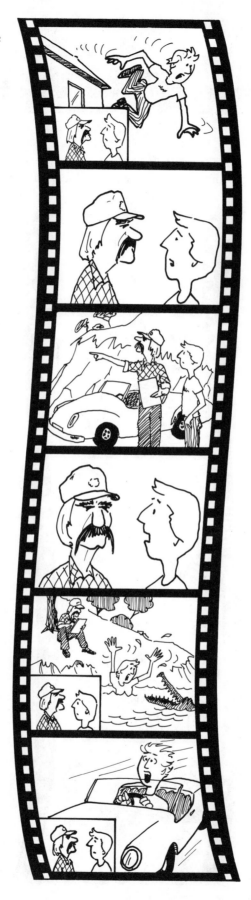

You FALL off the building. Remember that you NEED to look scared while you FALL.

—Oh, I REMEMBER.

—After that, we HAVE a car crash. You DRIVE this car off that cliff into the lake.

—Which car you DRIVE?

—I NOT DRIVE a car. I'm the stunt coordinator. Whenever you DO a stunt, I HAVE to watch and take notes. Now, let me explain this.

Be sure not to lose control of the car until you GO 80 miles per hour.

You*'ll hit* that rock, and
the car *will roll* over.

The car *will land* in the
lake and *start* to sink.
While it*'s sinking*, you*'re
going to crawl* out and
cling to the top of the car.

Make sure that you look
miserable while you*'re
clinging* to the car.

—Oh, that *won't be* hard.
I*'ll look* miserable.

—Good. Hmmm. Let me
see. What *are* we *doing*
next?

—We?

You HIT that rock, and
the car ROLL over.

The car LAND in the
lake and START to sink.
While it SINK, you
CRAWL out and CLING
to the top of the car.

Make sure that you look
miserable while you
CLING to the car.

—Oh, that NOT BE hard.
I LOOK miserable.

—Good. Hmmm. Let me
see. What we DO next?

—We?

—You. Ah, yes. You're *going to jog* down the street.

As you're *jogging*, a lion *will growl* at you from behind that tree.

It's important for you to look nervous while he's *attacking* you.

—Attacking me? Listen. I have my own plan for these stunts. I'm *not falling* off any building. I'm *not driving* a car off any cliff. And no lion *is attacking* me!

—Ah! Good! You're our new stunt person! You'll *be* pretty busy today. We're *going to begin* in about an hour.

THE END

—You. Ah, yes. You JOG down the street.

As you JOG, a lion GROWL at you from behind that tree.

It's important for you to look nervous while he ATTACK you.

—Attacking me? Listen. I have my own plan for these stunts. I NOT FALL off any building. I NOT DRIVE a car off any cliff. And no lion ATTACK me!

—Ah! Good! You're our new stunt person! You BE pretty busy today. We BEGIN in about an hour.

PRESENT CONTINUOUS	SIMPLE FUTURE: WILL/BE GOING TO

NOW   FUTURE

On a time line, the PRESENT CONTINUOUS (meaning the future) looks like the other future tenses. However, it is used differently.

1.	The PRESENT CONTINUOUS (meaning the future) is used for a *planned* future action or event. It is generally interchangeable with the BE GOING TO form.	BE GOING TO (but not WILL) is also used for a future *plan*.
	What *are* we *doing* next?	What *are* we *going to do* next?
	EXCEPTIONS: The PRESENT CON-TINUOUS is not used for the future with:	
	a. verbs such as *rain*, *snow*, *get sick*, or *die* because these aren't planned events, and	
	b. NON-ACTION verbs. (See the Appendix, page 155.)	
2.	In the negative, the PRESENT CONTINUOUS indicates:	In the negative, BE GOING TO indicates the negative of a plan for the future:
	a. the negative of a plan for the future:	
	He's *not coming* tomorrow.	He's *not going* to come tomorrow.
	b. refusal:	Both WILL and BE GOING TO are used for refusal:
	I'*m not driving* this car off that cliff. (= I refuse to drive this car off that cliff.)	I *won't drive* this car. = I'*m not going* to drive this car. (= I refuse to drive this car.)
3.	When the PRESENT CONTINUOUS means the future, some indication of time is given in either the sentence itself or in the whole context:	

—What *are* you *doing* tomorrow? (sentence) —I'*m starting* a new job as a stunt man. (context)	

| 4. | The PRESENT CONTINUOUS is often used in subordinate clauses that express *time* and *condition* with these words:

when
while
as (= while)
until
by the time
if
unless
in case

Whenever you'*re doing* a stunt, I'll have to watch and take notes.

You'll need to look scared while you'*re falling*.

NOTE: Sometimes the PRESENT CONTINUOUS is used in the main clause. When it is, some indication of time is usually in the sentence.

We'*re discussing* it tomorrow while we're driving to work. | We usually use WILL or BE GOING TO in the main clauses of sentences with subordinate clauses of time or condition.

Whenever you're doing a stunt, I'*ll have to watch* and take notes. |

FILL IT IN

DIRECTIONS: Fill in the blanks in the following story with the FUTURE TENSE (WILL or BE GOING TO) or the PRESENT CONTINUOUS. Remember that more than one tense may be possible in some of the blanks.

Johnny, the new stunt man, decided that he didn't like that business very much. He has now decided to learn to become a roofer.

THE ROOFING BUSINESS

—Johnny, you (1)_____ (really like) working with me. It

(2)_____ (be) a great opportunity for you to learn the trade. Let me explain what we (3)_____ (do) tomorrow. First, we (4)_____ (have to) load the

materials onto the truck at the warehouse. As you

(5)_____ (load) 50-pound rolls of roofing

paper onto the truck, I (6)_____ (count)

to make sure that you have 20. Then while you

(7)_____ (load) the buckets of nails, I

(8)_____ (watch) that you don't drop any.

After the nails are loaded, you (9)_____

(get) the tar machine started. While you

(10)_____ (do) that, I (11)_____ (get) some coffee and doughnuts.

We (12)_____ (finish) at the warehouse by 7 o'clock. I (13)_____

(read) the map along the way while you (14)_____ (drive) the truck. When we

arrive, you (15)_____ (unload) the truck, and I (16)_____ (ring) the

doorbell to announce our arrival. I (17)_____ (hold)

the ladder while you (18)_____ (carry) the rolls of

roofing paper and nails onto the roof. As you (19)_____

(spread) the tar on the roof, I (20)_____ (listen)

to make sure the machine doesn't stop. I (21)_____

(watch) you roll the paper to make sure that you

(22)_____ (roll) it straight. I (23)_____

(tell) you if it's crooked so that you (24)_____ (be)

able to fix it before the tar gets hard. While you

(25)_____ (finish) the roof, I (26)_____ (go) down to buy lunch. By

the time I come back, you'll be finished with the last

roll. Then I (27)_____ (hand) you the nails

while you (28)_____ (hammer) them in.

At 5 o'clock you (29)_____ (clean up). I

(30)_____ (tell) the people good-bye. Yes,

sir, tomorrow (31)_____ (be) a great day

for you. By the way, Johnny, (32)_____

(you go) to Joe's party tomorrow night?

　　—No, Jack, I think I (33)_____ (be) too tired.

　　—Don't worry, Johnny. When you have as much experience as I do, you

(34)_____ (not get) tired out so easily.

	Monday	Tuesday	Wednesday	Thursday	Friday
9:00	drive a car into the ocean	spread net across street		chase a thief	float down rapids on a raft
10:00	thrash about in water as if drowning		take flying lessons		dive off a cliff
11:00		climb skyscraper		run away from bears	
12:00	fight off sharks		fly plane over Himalayas		ride a motorcycle
1:00	go to seafood restaurant	fight criminal on skyscraper		shoot a lion	
2:00			crash plane into mountain		drown in lake
3:00	swim laps to get in shape		jump out of burning plane		
4:00	review film	jump off a building		do retakes of movie	swing across the jungle on a rope

DIRECTIONS: **A.** Above is the stunt man's schedule for next week. Ask your partner questions about the schedule using WILL/BE GOING TO or the PRESENT CONTINUOUS tense.

Examples: What is he going to do at ten o'clock on Monday?
    Where is he going at one o'clock on Monday?

B. Ask your partner questions about his or her week's schedule.

Example: What are you doing tomorrow at three o'clock?

16

DIRECTIONS: Read the following story. When you finish, go back to the beginning, cover up the story to the left, and choose the correct tense for each capitalized simple form of the verb to the right of the picture.

A
NEW
BROTHER

—Well, Heather, tomorrow we're *going to bring* your mother and new little brother, Timmy, home from the hospital.

—Well, Heather, tomorrow we BRING your mother and new little brother, Timmy, home from the hospital.

It's *going to be* wonderful having a new family member.

It BE wonderful having a new family member.

You'll *be helping* your mother take care of Timmy while he's *growing up.*

You HELP your mother take care of Timmy while he GROW UP.

He'll *grow* very quickly. When he is four months old, he'll *be rolling* over.

He GROW very quickly. When he is four months old, he ROLL over.

He*'ll be getting* his first cute little tooth at around six months.

He GET his first cute little tooth at around six months.

At seven months he*'ll be crawling*

At seven months he CRAWL.

Then he*'ll learn* to walk. While he*'s taking* his first step, we*'ll* all *be watching*.

Then he LEARN to walk. While he TAKE his first step, we all WATCH.

While he*'s learning* to walk, he*'ll be falling down* a lot.

While he LEARN to walk, he FALL DOWN a lot.

He*'ll fall down*, and you*'ll pick* him *up*.

He FALL DOWN, and you PICK UP him.

As he*'s getting* older, you*'ll be lending* him your toys.

As he GET older, you LEND him your toys.

He'll *wind up* your toys for you.

He WIND UP your toys for you.

You'll *be blowing up* balloons for him to play with.

You BLOW UP balloons for him to play with.

It *will be* fun having a brother to do things with.

It BE fun having a brother to do things with.

We'll *be taking* him to the beach often next summer. You'll *be teaching* him how to swim while we're there.

We TAKE him to the beach often next summer. You TEACH him how to swim while we're there.

He's *going to be watching* you while you're *building* sand castles.

He WATCH you while you BUILD sand castles.

You'll *build* sand castles, and then he'll *play* with them.

You BUILD sand castles, and then he PLAY with them.

We'll also *be taking* him to the park. He'll *go* down the slide and you'll *catch* him.

Then when he's *learning* to ride a bicycle, you'll *be running* alongside him.

Before too long, you're *going to be walking* him to school every day.

He'll *be drawing* lots of pictures all through elementary school, and you'll *be helping* him.

You're really *going to appreciate* having a younger brother, Heather. . . . Heather, where are you going?

THE END

We also TAKE him to the park. He GO down the slide and you CATCH him.

Then when he LEARN to ride a bicycle, you RUN alongside him.

Before too long, you WALK him to school every day.

He DRAW lots of pictures all through elementary school, and you HELP him.

You really APPRECIATE having a younger brother, Heather. . . . Heather, where are you going?

1.

There are two forms of the FUTURE CONTINUOUS:

will be (eating)
be going to be (eating)

These are generally interchangeable; however, the latter is rarely used because of its length.

See Chapter 13 for details.

2.

The FUTURE CONTINUOUS indicates an action that will be in progress at a definite time in the future.

Next month, he'll be crawling.
At midnight tomorrow, I'll be hiding under his crib.

When the action won't be repeated and will be at an indefinite or unknown future time, the SIMPLE FUTURE may also be used.

Soon he'll get his first tooth. =
Soon he'll be getting his first tooth.

3.

The FUTURE CONTINUOUS is also used for an action that will be in progress when another action happens.

While he's taking his first step, we'll be watching.

The SIMPLE FUTURE is used for a future action that will happen after another future action.

He'll fall down, and you'll pick him up.

4.

The FUTURE CONTINUOUS also emphasizes the (long) duration of a future action.

He'll be drawing all day long.

5.	The FUTURE CONTINUOUS is used for repeated future actions. ───────┬─── ×　×　×　×　×　× ────── 　　　　　NOW We'll *be taking* him there often.	
6.	The FUTURE CONTINUOUS is not used with NON-ACTION verbs. (See the Appendix, page 155.)	

The PRESENT CONTINUOUS (meaning the future) is often used in the subordinate clauses of sentences that have the FUTURE CONTINUOUS in the main clause.

Example:　　　While you*'re building* sand castles, he'll be watching.

To check the use of the PRESENT CONTINUOUS, refer to Chapters 1, 3, and 15.

PICTURE PUZZLE

DIRECTIONS:　Write out the following story on another piece of paper. Change the pictures and symbols to words. For each of the encircled verbs, choose the PRESENT CONTINUOUS (meaning the future), the SIMPLE FUTURE (WILL or BE GOING TO), or the FUTURE CONTINUOUS. In some cases, more than one tense may be possible. The main character is the child from the earlier story.

　　　　　😀 = I (OR ME)　　　🙂 = HE (OR HIM)

MY PLAN FOR MY NEW BROTHER

MY PARENTS (BRING) MY NEW BABY BROTHER 🏠 FROM THE 🏥 TOMORROW A.M. & LIFE (BE) JUST TERRIBLE FOR 😀. MY PARENTS (P̶A̶Y̶) ANY ATTENTION → 😀 ANYMORE. WHILE MY MOTHER (FEED) 🙂, 😀 (DO) MY HOMEWORK W/OUT ANY HELP. WHILE 😀 (READ) MY SCHOOL 📖s OUT LOUD, MY FATHER (L̶I̶S̶T̶E̶N̶) BECAUSE HE (PLAY) W/ MY BABY BROTHER. WHILE 😀 (SWING) ☒ THE BACKYARD, MY BROTHER (CRAWL) ACROSS THE LAWN, SO MY PARENTS (WATCH) ME. AS MY BROTHER (GROW) ↑, 😀 (SHRINK) ☒→ THE BACKGROUND.

HOWEVER, 😀 HAVE A PLAN. @ (🕖) TOMORROW 🌙✶, 😀 (HIDE) 🖥 MY BROTHER'S

[bed], & [baby] (WAIT) UNTIL MY PARENTS (SLEEP). THEN [face] (GRAB) MY BROTHER &
QUIETLY (CREEP) [out] OF THE [house]. [face] (GET) [box] A [bus] & TAKE [him] BACK → THE
[HOSPITAL]. [face] (TRADE) [him] [x] [box] SOMETHING ELSE: MAYBE A [dog] OR A [horse] OR A [robot].

[box] THE OTHER [hand], MAYBE [face] (STEAL) [him]. IF [face] DO, THE POLICE (PROBABLY ARREST)
[face] FOR KIDNAPPING. MY MOTHER (PROBABLY FAINT), & MY FATHER (YELL) A LOT &
(TEAR) [out] HIS HAIR. NO, [face] (~~TRADE~~) [him] [x]. INSTEAD, [face] (TEACH) [him] THINGS. FOR
EXAMPLE, [face] (TEACH) [him] → PLAY HIDE & SEEK. WHILE [face] (HIDE), [him] (LOOK) FOR [face].
AND [face] (TEACH) [him] → RIDE A [bicycle] & BUILD A TOY [house] & FLOAT [x] THE [boat]. [face] (TEACH)
[him] ABOUT THE [zoo animals] [x] THE ZOO, TOO. OF COURSE, WHILE [him] (LEARN) ALL THESE
THINGS, MY PARENTS (IGNORE) [face]. [face] (TEACH) [him] ALL [day] LONG, BUT MY PARENTS
(PROBABLY THINK) HE'S A GENIUS.

[face] KNOW WHAT [face] (DO). [face] (RUN) AWAY FROM [house]! ONE [night], WHEN MY
PARENTS (SLEEP), [face] (PACK) MY [suitcase] & QUIETLY (CREEP) [out] OF THE [house]. [face] (GET) [box]
A [bus] & (LEAVE) THE [city] FAR BEHIND. WHILE MY LITTLE BROTHER (GROW) ↑, [him]
(WISH) HE HAD A BIG SISTER → TEACH [him] ABOUT [bicycle]s & [boat]s & [zoo animal]s
& PARENTS!

RAP IT UP

DIRECTIONS: **A.** Use the following time expressions and the verb phrases from Part B to make up sentences about Timmy's family. Use the FUTURE CONTINUOUS tense.

Example: At 9:00 tomorrow morning, Timmy's father will be changing Timmy's diaper.

TIME EXPRESSIONS

9:00 tomorrow morning	1:00 Monday morning
dinner time	the day after tomorrow at 6:00
12:30 Saturday afternoon	breakfast time
next Thursday evening at 7:00	11:00 tomorrow night
8:00 tomorrow evening	after lunch

B. Combine two phrases from the following list to make sentences telling what Timmy's family will be doing. Use the PRESENT CONTINUOUS and the FUTURE CONTINUOUS. Also, use words such as: *while, as,* and *when.*

Example: As Timmy's mother is rocking him, she will be singing.

VERB PHRASES

change diapers	play ball with him	do homework
bathe him	listen to music	read the newspaper
feed him	teach him to walk	give him his vitamins
take pictures of him	wash bottles	rock him
sing	watch television	read to him
dress him	wash his clothes	talk on the telephone
rest	comb his hair	watch him crawl
take him swimming	pick him up	push him in stroller

C. Choose one of the following things that could change your life. Pretend it's going to happen to you very soon. Tell what you'll be doing during the next year.

---

take care of your 6-year-old nephew for a year
work as a jewel thief
work in the zoo taking care of the animals
make movies
travel into space
buy a house that needs repair work
get married
have a baby
win a lot of money
become president

DIRECTIONS: Read the story on the left. When you finish, go back to the beginning, cover up the story to the left, and choose the correct tense for each capitalized simple form of the verb to the right of the picture.

THE PLANS OF A JUNIOR GENIUS

—I've always believed that it's important to plan for the future. I've been putting together some ideas for my "Life Schedule."

When I *graduate* from elementary school next month, I'*m going to celebrate* because I *will have finished* my first six years of school.

By graduation day, I *will have learned* to play chess.

I also *will have done* a lot of experiments with my chemistry set and then *gotten* bored with it.

—I've always believed that it's important to plan for the future. I've been putting together some ideas for my "Life Schedule."

When I GRADUATE from elementary school next month, I CELEBRATE because I FINISH my first six years of school.

By graduation day, I LEARN to play chess.

I also DO a lot of experiments with my chemistry set and then GET bored with it.

By the time I *finish* high school, I *will have taken* algebra, geometry, and calculus.

I'*ll* probably *give* the graduation speech because I *will have gotten* straight A's all through high school.

By graduation day, I *will have completed* my independent studies of animal behavior.

When I *graduate* from college, I'*ll get* a job as a math teacher.

By that time, I *will have become* the university chess champion and a computer expert.

When I *turn* 30, I'*m going to start* making plans for a new career because I probably *will have gotten* bored with my life.

By the time I FINISH high school, I TAKE algebra, geometry, and calculus.

I probably GIVE the graduation speech because I GET straight A's all through high school.

By graduation day, I COMPLETE my independent studies of animal behavior.

When I GRADUATE from college, I GET a job as a math teacher.

By that time, I BECOME the university chess champion and a computer expert.

When I TURN 30, I START making plans for a new career because I probably GET bored with my life.

I *will have taught* math at several universities. . .

I TEACH math at several universities. . .

. . .and *written* a lot of texts.

. . . and WRITE a lot of texts.

I hope that by that time I *will have won* an international chess tournament.

I hope that by that time I WIN an international chess tournament.

It*'ll be* time to move on to something completely new.

It BE time to move on to something completely new.

I think I*'m going to go* to Africa and *study* the animals there.

I think I GO to Africa and STUDY the animals there.

By the time I *come* home from my first safari, I *will have captured* thousands of creatures on film. . .

By the time I COME home from my first safari, I CAPTURE thousands of creatures on film. . .

. . . and I *will have gathered* a lot of information on wild animal behavior.

When my book of African photographs *is* published, I'*ll become* world famous.

Maybe I'*ll* even *win* awards for my genius with a camera.

—Billy, it's time to put away your toys and go to bed.

—When *is* the world *going to learn* to appreciate genius?

THE END

. . . and I GATHER a lot of information on wild animal behavior.

When my book of African photographs BE published, I BECOME world famous.

Maybe I EVEN WIN awards for my genius with a camera.

—Billy, it's time to put away your toys and go to bed.

—When the world LEARN to appreciate genius?

1.	The FUTURE PERFECT expresses an action that will end *before* another action in the future. That is, we use the FUTURE PERFECT when we "jump back" from another future time. ———┃——————┃——————✕ NOW FUTURE FUTURE PERFECT When I turn 30, I *will have gotten* bored with my life. (NOTE: *when = before*)	We usually use the SIMPLE FUTURE if we move "forward" in time and if it is clear which action happened first.  NOW FUTURE When I turn 30, I'*m going to start* making plans for a new career. (NOTE: *when = when* or *after*)
2.	The FUTURE PERFECT doesn't always begin in the future. ◄——┃——————┃——————✕ PAST NOW FUTURE When he retires next year, he *will have worked* here for 35 years. In this case, because the duration of time is emphasized, we often use the FUTURE PERFECT CONTINUOUS instead. (See Chapter 18.)	(For details on the SIMPLE FUTURE, see Chapter 13.)

The SIMPLE PRESENT (meaning the future) is often used in the subordinate clauses of sentences that have the FUTURE PERFECT in the main clause.

Example: When I *graduate* from college, I will have read every available book on higher mathematics.

The PRESENT PERFECT (meaning the future) is also sometimes used in the subordinate clause.

To check the use of the SIMPLE PRESENT, refer to Chapters 1, 2, and 14.

DIRECTIONS: Fill in the blanks in the following story with the FUTURE PERFECT, SIMPLE FUTURE, or SIMPLE PRESENT. Remember that more than one tense may be possible in some of the blanks.

MRS. ADAMS'S CLASS

It's another first day of school—the twentieth first day for Mrs. Adams, the third-grade teacher. The school year no longer holds any surprises for her. She knows that by the end of the first day, at least two kids (1)_____ (run) home crying. Someone (2)_____ (stick) gum in the drinking fountain, and someone else (3)_____ (fall) asleep during her "first-day-of-school" lecture. By the time the final bell (4)_____ (ring), one or two kids (5)_____ (lose) their new notebooks. Several more (6)_____ (tear) their new school clothes.

The first week (7)_____ (finally come) to an end, and then it (8)_____ (be) time for serious business. By the end of the first month, Mrs. Adams (9)_____ (hear) at least thirty different excuses for incomplete homework. At least half a dozen kids (10)_____ (not understand) three-fourths of the lessons. She (11)_____ (explain) the same points at least ten times each.

When Halloween (12)_____ (arrive), over half the class (13)_____ (get) sick from eating too much candy. It (14)_____ (take) at least a week before they (15)_____ (recover).

By Christmas, one-fourth of the students (16)_____ (fail) half the tests. After they (17)_____ (fail), all of them (18)_____ (promise) to do a better job during the new year.

When spring vacation (19)_____ (roll around), everyone (20)_____ (be) ready for a break. The students (21)_____ (complain) over and over about Mrs. Adams being too strict. They (22)_____ (get) tired of doing homework. Mrs. Adams (23)_____ (be) ready for her annual week at the health spa where she

(24)_____ (sit) in the sauna and (25)_____ (sweat) out

all her problems.

When they (26)_____ (return) to school after spring break, the students

(27)_____ (forget) everything they learned before the vacation. It

(28)_____ (take) two weeks to return to normal.

By June, Mrs. Adams (29)_____ (consider) retiring several times. She

(30)_____ (swear) to quit at least two dozen times. But we all know that when

school (31)_____ (begin) again next September, she (32)_____ (be)

there ready for her new group of little "geniuses."

RAP IT UP

DIRECTIONS: **A.** Below are some of the students in Billy's class. In the middle column are things they are going to do next year. In the column on the right are things they will have done by the time of their ten-year class reunion. Make sentences using the SIMPLE FUTURE and the FUTURE PERFECT.

Examples: Jason is going to begin lifting weights next year.
By the ten-year reunion, he will have won 3 Olympic gold medals for weightlifting.

	Next year	By 10-year reunion
Jason	begin lifting weights	win 3 Olympic gold medals for weightlifting
Brock	get braces	become a famous model
Kevin	take singing lessons	become an opera star
Georgette	study chemistry	discover a cure for a rare disease
Chester	get a puppy for his birthday	become a lion tamer
Debbie	begin exercising	open her own health spa
Mark	take swimming lessons	swim the English Channel
Heidi	begin sailing lessons	sail around the world
Theodore	climb trees with a friend	climb Mt. Everest
Amanda	practice writing	become a famous novelist

B. Fill in your "life schedule" below. Use your imagination. In a group of three students, exchange your life schedules. Student A will ask Student B about Student C, Student B will ask Student C about Student A, and so on.

Example: —In five years, how many places will he have traveled to?
              —He will have traveled to three different places.

	Next month	Next year	In 5 years	In 10 years
career	_____	_____	_____	_____
hobby	_____	_____	_____	_____
love life	_____	_____	_____	_____
travel	_____	_____	_____	_____
personal appearance	_____	_____	_____	_____

C. Predict world events that will begin in the year 2500 or will have happened by then. Use the SIMPLE FUTURE and the FUTURE PERFECT.

DIRECTIONS: Read the story on the left. When you finish, go back to the beginning, cover up the story to the left, and choose the correct tense for each capitalized simple form of the verb to the right of the picture.

LIFE
IN A
DIVING
BELL

Dear Mom,
  Guess what? We've finally figured out a way to get letters to the top. By the time you *receive* this letter, we *will have been living* in this diving bell for three years.

You *will be shaking* your head as you *read* this and *wondering* how I could consent to live under the ocean.

But, really, it's not as hard as you may think. By fall of next year we *will have been conducting* scientific research here for almost 4 years.

Besides, it's good to know that when we *leave* here we *won't have been wasting* the last few years; instead, we *will have been helping* to make humankind's knowledge of the marine world more complete.

Dear Mom,
  Guess what? We've finally figured out a way to get letters to the top. By the time you RECEIVE this letter, we LIVE in this diving bell for three years.

You SHAKE your head as you READ this and WONDER how I could consent to live under the ocean.

But, really, it's not as hard as you may think. By fall of next year we CONDUCT scientific research here for almost 4 years.

Besides, it's good to know that when we LEAVE here we NOT WASTE the last few years; instead, we HELP to make humankind's knowledge of the marine world more complete.

Our life in this little "cell" has now become almost routine. For example, tomorrow Leonard *will be working* outside on the ocean floor as usual.

He *is going to be planting* the crops.

Of course, farming is not the only thing he *will be doing* tomorrow. He *will be exploring* parts of the ocean that are new to him and *searching* for new species of fish and plant life.

Here in the ocean he's not only a scientist and farmer; he's also a hunter. He hunts fish for food every day.

I worry about him because I know that by the time he *gets* home tomorrow evening, he *will have been fighting off* sharks all day in order to provide food for us.

It's good to know that when we *come* up for Thanksgiving next month, we *will be eating* turkey instead of fish.

Our life in this little "cell" has now become almost routine. For example, tomorrow Leonard WORK outside on the ocean floor as usual.

He PLANT the crops.

Of course, farming is not the only thing he DO tomorrow. He EXPLORE parts of the ocean that are new to him and SEARCH for new species of fish and plant life.

Here in the ocean he's not only a scientist and farmer; he's also a hunter. He hunts fish for food every day.

I worry about him because I know that by the time he GET home tomorrow evening, he FIGHT OFF sharks all day in order to provide food for us.

It's good to know that when we COME up for Thanksgiving next month, we EAT turkey instead of fish.

By that time I *will have been dreaming* about meat, French fries, and hot fudge sundaes for 3 years.

To help pass the time between now and then, I'*ll be fixing* seaweed cakes to bring up with us.

I *am* also *going to be training* some dolphins to help protect us and our home.

They *will be guarding* our cell from any intruders.

You *will be wondering* by now about this cell we call home.

It is a fairly small one, with room only for a bed, a table, and a small area for exercising.

By that time I DREAM about meat, French fries, and hot fudge sundaes for 3 years.

To help pass the time between now and then, I FIX seaweed cakes to bring up with us.

I also TRAIN some dolphins to help protect us and our home.

They GUARD our cell from any intruders.

You WONDER by now about this cell we call home.

It is a fairly small one, with room only for a bed, a table, and a small area for exercising.

Soon, we *are going to be building* a new, more roomy place to live in.

When we *come* up, we *will be looking* for building materials.

We'll also *be shopping* for clothes for the three of us.

Yes, mother, we have a little surprise for you.

On Thanksgiving you *will be meeting* Erica, your new granddaughter.
Love,
Rebecca

Soon, we BUILD a new, more roomy place to live. in.

When we COME up, we LOOK for building materials.

We also SHOP for clothes for the three of us.

Yes, mother, we have a little surprise for you.

On Thanksgiving you MEET Erica, your new granddaughter.
Love,
Rebecca

THE END

FUTURE PERFECT CONTINUOUS | FUTURE CONTINUOUS

1.

The FUTURE PERFECT CONTIN-UOUS emphasizes the (long) duration of an action or a habitual action *before* another time in the future. The length of time is usually given in the sentence. We often use *for* or *since* with the FUTURE PERFECT CONTINUOUS.

By the time you receive this, we *will have been living* here for three years.

The FUTURE CONTINUOUS emphasizes the duration of an action or a habitual action *at* or *after* another future time.

You*'ll be shaking* your head as you read this.

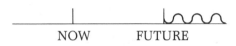

When we come, we*'ll be shopping* for building materials.

2.

The FUTURE PERFECT CONTIN-UOUS may begin at any time *before* the other future action; it may even begin in the past. Again, the length of time is usually given, often with *for* or *since*.

I *will have been dreaming* about hot fudge sundaes for three years.

The FUTURE CONTINUOUS may be used alone, without another future time in the sentence. In this way, we may use the word *for* to indicate the length of time.

We*'ll be staying* with you for several weeks.

However, we do not use *since* with the FUTURE CONTINUOUS.

(For more on the FUTURE CON-TINUOUS see Chapter 16.)

3.

We don't use either the FUTURE PERFECT CONTINUOUS or the FUTURE CONTINUOUS with NON-ACTION verbs. (See the Appendix, page 155.)

4.

The SIMPLE PRESENT (meaning the future) is often used in the subordinate clauses of sentences that have the FUTURE PERFECT CONTINUOUS in the main clause.

By the time you *receive* this, we will have been living here for three years.

To check the usage of the SIMPLE PRESENT, refer to Chapters 1, 2, and 14.

DIRECTIONS: On another piece of paper, write out the following story. Change the pictures and symbols to words. For each of the encircled verbs, choose the SIMPLE PRESENT, FUTURE CONTINUOUS, or FUTURE PERFECT CONTINUOUS. In a few cases more than tense may be possible.

This is a letter to Rebecca (the woman in the diving bell earlier in this chapter) from her mother.

A VISIT FROM REBECCA AND LEONARD

DEAR REBECCA,

WHEN YOU (COME) ↑ [□↗] OF YOUR [diving bell] ⊠ A FEW WEEKS, YOUR FATHER & I (WAIT) FOR YOU [↑] THE [boat]. BY THAT TIME, WE (LOOK FORWARD) → YOUR VISIT FOR 4 YEARS — EVER SINCE YOU CHOSE THIS STRANGE LINE OF WORK & WENT ↓ THERE.

WHILE WE (WAIT) ABOARD THE [boat], YOUR BROTHERS & SISTERS (DECORATE) THE [house] & (FIX) AN ENORMOUS MEAL (W/OUT ANY [fish] AT ALL). AS WE (DRIVE) [house], THEY (PREPARE) YOUR FAVORITE FOODS, & YOUR NIECES & NEPHEWS (CHASE) EACH OTHER [□], (STICK) THEIR [finger]S ⊠→ THE [cake], & (PULL) THE [dog]'S TAIL. WHEN WE (ARRIVE) [house], THEY ALL (STAND) [↑] THE FRONT PORCH. AFTER EVERYONE (HUG) & (KISS), WE (CATCH) ↑ [↑] THE NEWS ALL WEEKEND.

WHEN YOU & LEONARD (GET) → THE SURFACE, YOU (HAVE) MEETINGS W/ FAMOUS SCIENTISTS FROM ALL [↑] THE [globe], & [newspaper] REPORTERS (INTERVIEW) YOU BECAUSE YOU (DO) IMPORTANT EXPERIMENTS & (DISCOVER) NEW SPECIES OF [fish]. UNFORTUNATELY, I (DO̶) ANYTHING VERY INTERESTING. I JUST (WASH) [dishes], (BALANCE) THE BUDGET, (TEAR) [□↗] COUPONS FROM THE [newspaper], & (TRY) → FIGURE [□↗] HOW → PERSUADE YOU → COME ↑ [□↗] OF YOUR [diving bell] & STAY W/ US [↑] DRY LAND.

LOVE,

Mom

LEONARD AND REBECCA'S CALENDAR FOR NEXT YEAR

	Jan.	Feb.	March	April	May	June	July	Aug.	Sept.	Oct.	Nov.	Dec.
Leonard	start exploring the ocean	start laboratory experiments		gather fossils	start taking photos	write reports			start building a new cell		freeze samples of fish	
Rebecca	start writing in her diary		sew new clothes	start treasure hunting			bake bread	start training dolphins			start preparing for Christmas	

DIRECTIONS: **A.** Work with a partner. Use the calendar above to ask and answer questions about Leonard and Rebecca's activities in the diving bell. Use the FUTURE CONTINUOUS and FUTURE PERFECT CONTINUOUS tenses in your questions and answers.

Examples: —What will Leonard be doing in May?
—He will be gathering fossils in May.
—By December how long will he have been taking photographs?
—By December he will have been taking photos for 6 months.

B. Make your own calendar for next year like the one above. Exchange with your partner and ask each other questions using the FUTURE CONTINUOUS and FUTURE PERFECT CONTINUOUS tenses. You may ask questions that bring in information not on the calendar.

DIRECTIONS: Fill in the blanks in the following story with the tenses below. In some cases, more than one tense is possible.

SIMPLE PRESENT (present and future)   FUTURE CONTINUOUS
PRESENT CONTINUOUS (present and future)   FUTURE PERFECT
SIMPLE FUTURE (will/be going to)   FUTURE PERFECT CONTINUOUS

A TRIP THROUGH TIME

Tomorrow Norman Norris, the world-famous explorer, (1)_____ (lead) an expedition into the future. This (2)_____ (be) Norman's last expedition because he (3)_____ (retire) next month. By that time, he (4)_____ (explore) not only every corner of the earth in our time, but he (5)_____ (also see) over twenty-five different centuries.

He (6)_____ (especially look) forward to tomorrow's trip because it (7)_____ (take) him and the other members of the expedition to the year 3000. That (8)_____ (be) the farthest anyone has ever traveled in the time rocket.

Norman and his crew members (9)_____ (work) twelve hours a day right now to prepare for the journey. They (10)_____ (stay) in shape by jogging. They (11)_____ (study) scientific material and (12)_____ (prepare) all of the cameras and equipment. They (13)_____ (take) lots of photographs during their trip. If the photographs (14)_____ (turn out) well, they (15)_____ (be) the first ones ever brought back.

The rocket (16)_____ (leave) at 6:00 tomorrow morning. During the flight, the crew (17)_____ (check) the calendar clock every few minutes to make sure that they (18)_____ (not pass) their destination.

The rocket's first stop (19)_____ (be) the year 2300. While the crew (20)_____ (visit) that time period, they (21)_____ (photograph) the people, animals, and buildings. As they (22)_____ (film) a space station, there (23)_____ (be) an attack from an enemy planet whose people (24)_____ (think) it (25)_____ (be) a military installation. The space station (26)_____ (catch) on fire. As they (27)_____ (watch) the burning station, a woman (28)_____ (scream), "My robot is inside." Then Norman

(29)_____ (run) into the burning station to rescue the robot. The crew

(30)_____ (film) as a terrified Norman (31)_____ (run) out with the

robot. As the woman (32)_____ (thank)

Norman, the robot (33)_____ (spin) around

and (34)_____ (bite) Norman on the nose.

At that moment, Norman (35)_____

(promise) himself that he (36)_____ (never

rescue) another robot for anyone.

　　During the stop in 2502, Norman (37)_____

(visit) a girlfriend from a previous time expedition. When

he (38)_____ (find) her, she (39)_____ (flirt)

with another man. Norman (40)_____ (get) very jealous and (41)_____

(start) a fight with the man. The man (42)_____ (punch) Norman in the nose,

which by this time (43)_____ (just recover) from the robot bite. Norman

(44)_____ (promise) himself that he (45)_____ (never fall) in love

again.

　　After they (46)_____ (arrive) in the year 3000, Norman (47)_____

(conduct) experiments on the environment for several weeks. He (48)_____ (study)

the plants and new species of animals that he (49)_____ (find). One day, while he

(50)_____ (do) his research, a group of strange people (51)_____

(kidnap) him and (52)_____ (take) him to their village. At first, he

(53)_____ (try) to escape. But the villagers (54)_____ (not let) him go.

While he (55)_____ (try) to crawl away, they (56)_____ (watch), and

they (57)_____ (bring) him back. He

(58)_____ (attempt) to escape thirty-five

times when he (59)_____ (meet) the

beautiful Zark. In spite of his promise to himself,

Norman (60)_____ (fall) in love again. He

(61)_____ (not return) to his time. He

(62)_____ (live) happily ever after in the

thirty-first century with Zark. How (63)_____

(I know) all of this (64)_____ (happen)? My name

(65)_____ (be) Zark.

DIRECTIONS: Use the phrases and pictures on this page to help you rewrite Norman's story. DO NOT LOOK BACK AT THE ORIGINAL STORY. Your story won't be exactly the same as the original, but you should correctly use all of the future tenses and the two present tenses. The verbs on this page are in either picture form or the simple form, but you will choose from the following tenses when you rewrite the story on the next page: SIMPLE FUTURE, FUTURE CONTINUOUS, FUTURE PERFECT, FUTURE PERFECT CONTINUOUS, SIMPLE PRESENT, and PRESENT CONTINUOUS.

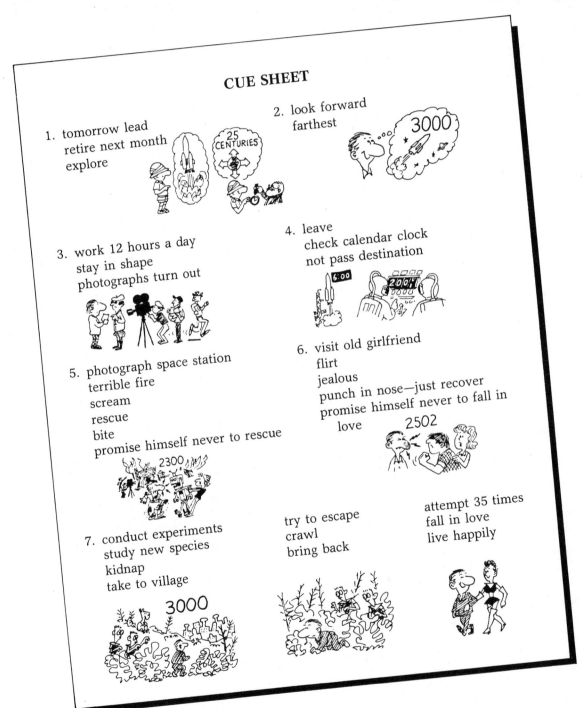

CUE SHEET

1. tomorrow lead
   retire next month
   explore

2. look forward
   farthest

3. work 12 hours a day
   stay in shape
   photographs turn out

4. leave
   check calendar clock
   not pass destination

5. photograph space station
   terrible fire
   scream
   rescue
   bite
   promise himself never to rescue

6. visit old girlfriend
   flirt
   jealous
   punch in nose—just recover
   promise himself never to fall in
   love

   try to escape
   crawl
   bring back

   attempt 35 times
   fall in love
   live happily

7. conduct experiments
   study new species
   kidnap
   take to village

A TRIP THROUGH TIME

The world-famous explorer, Norman Norris, is going to lead an expedition into the future tomorrow.

DIRECTIONS: **A.** Use the following story line to help you answer the questions on the next page. This story line tells you what will happen during Norman and Zark's honeymoon. The verbs on this page are all in the simple form. You should use the correct tense.

NORMAN AND ZARK'S HONEYMOON

NOW	TOMORROW	2ⁿᵈ DAY
• READ TRAVEL BOOKS • BUY NEW CLOTHES • STUDY MAP • PACK SUITCASE	• RENT A SUPER-TERRESTRIAL VEHICLE • 8:00 A.M. — BEGIN TRIP • DRIVE ALL DAY • 5:00 P.M. — REACH MOTEL AT BEACH	• 12:00 — 4:00 LIE ON BEACH • NORMAN TOO SUNBURNED TO SLEEP

3ʳᵈ DAY	4ᵗʰ DAY	5ᵗʰ DAY
• GO DIVING • NORMAN - HIT NOSE ON OCEAN FLOOR • ZARK - SWIM OVER TO HELP	• GO TO BEACH • NORMAN — LIE UNDER BEACH UMBRELLA ALL DAY • ZARK - SWIM WITH DOLPHINS	• NORMAN - SWIM • SHARK BITE NORMAN'S NOSE • ZARK — SCREAM

6ᵗʰ DAY	7ᵗʰ DAY	8ᵗʰ DAY
• NORMAN - FLOAT IN RAFT • PASSING FISHERMAN THROW OUT FISH ATTRACTING DEVICE, HIT NORMAN ON NOSE	• NORMAN — WATCH SUPER-MARINE VEHICLE RACES • BEE STING HIM ON NOSE	• NORMAN - LIE UNDER PALM TREE • COCONUT FALL ON HIS NOSE

9ᵗʰ DAY	10ᵗʰ DAY	11ᵗʰ DAY
• 10:00 - NORMAN AND ZARK BEGIN BUILDING SAND CASTLE • 2:30 - ROBOT KNOCK OVER SAND CASTLE • NORMAN — CHASE ROBOT • ZARK - LAUGH AT NORMAN AND ROBOT	• NORMAN AND ZARK WALK HAND IN HAND ON BEACH • EAT NUTRITION CAPSULES • TAKE NAP IN AFTERNOON • GO DANCING	• GO HOME • SCHEDULE NOSE SURGERY

B. Look at the story line on the previous page and answer these questions. Use the following tenses: SIMPLE PRESENT (present and future), PRESENT CONTINUOUS (present and future), SIMPLE FUTURE (will/be going to), FUTURE CONTINUOUS, FUTURE PERFECT, and FUTURE PERFECT CONTINUOUS.

1. What are Norman and Zark doing to prepare for their trip?
2. What time are they leaving tomorrow?
3. What's the first thing they're going to do tomorrow morning?
4. How many hours will they have been driving when they arrive at their motel?
5. How long will they lie on the beach on the second day?
6. Why won't Norman be able to sleep on the second night?
7. How many days will they have been on their honeymoon when they go diving?
8. What's going to happen to Norman when he's diving?
9. What is Zark going to do when Norman hits his nose?
10. Why won't Norman get sunburned on the fourth day?
11. What will Zark be doing while Norman is lying under the beach umbrella?
12. What is Norman going to be doing when the shark bites him?
13. What will Zark do when the shark bites Norman?
14. What is Norman doing on the sixth day?
15. What will happen when the fisherman throws out his bait bucket?
16. What will Norman be doing when the bee stings him on the nose?
17. What is Norman going to be doing when the coconut hits him?
18. By the eighth day, how many days will Norman have lain on the beach?
19. How long will Norman have been building his sand castle when the robot knocks it over?
20. What will Zark have been doing?
21. What will Norman do after the robot knocks down his sand castle?
22. What will Zark do?
23. What are Norman and Zark going to do on the tenth day?
24. What are they eating for lunch that day?
25. What will they do after lunch?
26. What will they be doing that evening?
27. What are they doing on the eleventh day?
28. How many times will Norman have hurt his nose by the time he gets home?
29. How many days will they have been honeymooning?
30. What's the first thing Norman's going to do when he gets home?

IT'S YOUR TURN: **A.** You are accompanying Norman on his expedition to the year 3000. Tell what you'll be doing. You are the filmmaker, pilot, cook, robot, and so on.

B. Someone has just told you that you can do or be anything you want. Anything is possible. Tell what you'll do and what your life is going to be like. Use *all* future tenses.

Examples: I'm going to learn to fly a jet.
    By the time I'm 40, I will have become president.

20

CUMULATIVE REVIEW

DIRECTIONS: In the following story, fill in the blanks with the tenses listed below.

SIMPLE PRESENT (present and future)
PRESENT CONTINUOUS (present and future)
SIMPLE PAST
PAST CONTINUOUS
PRESENT PERFECT
PRESENT PERFECT CONTINUOUS
PAST PERFECT

PAST PERFECT CONTINUOUS
FUTURE IN THE PAST
FUTURE (*will/be going to*)
FUTURE CONTINUOUS
FUTURE PERFECT
FUTURE PERFECT CONTINUOUS

AN INTERESTING EVENING

I.

Dear Mom and Dad,

I am having a wonderful time in this country. There are so many new things to see and do. And the people I (1)_____ (meet) are so interesting and charming that I want to take this opportunity to tell you all about them.

The excitement (2)_____ (begin) on the ship on the way over. There I (3)_____ (meet) my first two friends, Sam and his partner Charlie. They (4)_____ (just return) from exploring the Himalayas. One evening they (5)_____ (tell) me all about their amazing adventure. It seems that in the beginning they (6)_____ (start) hiking on the weekends simply for relaxation. On the first few trips they (7)_____ (make) many mistakes. Of course at that time, one of them (8)_____ (be) overweight and the other in bad shape. More than once they (9)_____ (think) of quitting. However, they (10)_____ (both be) reluctant to give up. After several months they (11)_____ (become) expert mountain climbers. They soon (12)_____ (become) world famous for climbing even the most difficult mountains. One day a rich businessman (13)_____ (ask) Sam and Charlie to lead a climbing expedition up the Himalayas. He (14)_____ (provide) them with a generous budget and all the able-bodied men they (15)_____ (need) to conduct their expedition. While they (16)_____ (climb), they (17)_____ (have) a lot of problems. Sam almost (18)_____ (fall) off a cliff, and Charlie almost (19)_____ (fall) into a crater. However, they (20)_____ (finally manage) to make it to the top. Sam and Charlie (21)_____ (tell) me that once they (22)_____ (reach) the top, they (23)_____ (find) some rare markings on

148 TENSE SITUATIONS

the rocks. It is unbelievable, but the markings seemed to be on the walls of the ruins of an old village.

Sam and Charlie are not the only interesting people I (24)_____ (meet) since I (25)_____ (leave) home. One night I (26)_____ (attend) a party given by Frankie, a classmate of mine. I (27)_____ (not know) that Frankie was really a famous rock star. When Frankie was young, he (28)_____ (want) to be a rock star. He (29)_____ (think) that he (30)_____ (be) rich and famous. He (31)_____ (dream) that people (32)_____ (follow) him and (33)_____ (beg) him for autographs. He (34)_____ (think) that he (35)_____ (spend) his summers lying on a beach on the Riviera. Frankie is famous now, but he is not happy. He (36)_____ (spend) his days trying to get away from people with autograph books. His summers (37)_____ (be) so busy that he (38)_____ (forget) to go to the beach. But Frankie (39)_____ (try) to change his life again. He (40)_____ (attend) classes at the university and (41)_____ (take) such courses as algebra, geometry, and calculus. He (42)_____ (plan) to become an engineer. When he (43)_____ (finish) school, he (44)_____ (move) to a country where they (45)_____ (not know) him and (46)_____ (lead) a quiet life.

II.

Also at the party there (47)_____ (be) another well-known person, this year's Miss America. She (48)_____ (be) a gorgeous girl and (49)_____ (be) everyone's favorite at the party. She was there with a charming foreign ambassador. Contrary to what you may think, she (50)_____ (not always be) this way. She (51)_____ (say) that at one time she had been a shy, unhappy young woman. Then she (52)_____ (become) a member of a health club. The owner, Harry, (53)_____ (inspire) her to jog, exercise, and get in shape. She (54)_____ (do) just that since she (55)_____ (meet) Harry. By November of this year, she (56)_____ (follow) his advice for three years. Nowadays she (57)_____ (not waste) any time. She (58)_____ (get up) every morning and (59)_____ (run) for five miles, then (60)_____ (swim) twenty laps in the pool. Her schedule (61)_____ (be) strict for these past few years, but it has been rewarding. Yes, Ellen Wiggley is a very happy person today.

I (62)_____ (find out) halfway through the evening that the purpose of the party was to raise money for Laura Kent's presidential campaign. I (63)_____ (see) her posters all over town, so I (64)_____ (recognize) her as soon as she (65)_____ (walk) in. She (66)_____ (shake) hands with all the guests before she (67)_____ (begin) her speech. If she (68)_____ (win) this election, she (69)_____ (provide) jobs for the needy and food for the hungry. She (70)_____ (say) she (71)_____ (balance) the budget and (72)_____ (improve) the economy. Everyone (73)_____ (applaud) when Mrs. Kent (74)_____ (promise): "I (75)_____ (not let) our country be pulled into war. I (76)_____ (not rest) until there is peace on this planet. I (77)_____ (promote) understanding among all people."

III.

She (78)_____ (finish) her speech when suddenly the doors (79)_____ (burst) open and the police (80)_____ (rush) in. The policemen (81)_____ (grab) the man who (82)_____ (flirt) with Ellen. When the commotion (83)_____ (begin), I (84)_____ (talk) to the man next to me. We (85)_____ (stop) talking when we (86)_____ (see) the police. Ellen (87)_____ (faint) when the police (88)_____ (arrest) the man beside her. While they (89)_____ (take) him away, one of the policemen (90)_____ (tell) us his story. The man was the internationally known spy Dudley Dangerfield. Dudley (91)_____ (work) as a spy for many years when he was suddenly fired by the only country that (92)_____ (not already fire) him. He (93)_____ (have) one misadventure after another in his career. In recent years he (94)_____ (fill) out one job application after another with no luck. Poor Dangerfield (95)_____ (starve) for months when he (96)_____ (decide) his only choice was a life of crime. The police (97)_____ (catch) him shoplifting several times when they (98)_____ (discover) his true identity.

I (99)_____ (really feel) very sorry for him when the man next to me (100)_____ (tell) me not to worry. He (101)_____ (introduce) himself as Johnny, an employment counselor. He (102)_____ (decide) to become a counselor because he (103)_____ (know) so much about different occupations. He himself (104)_____ (work) at all kinds of different jobs. For example, he (105)_____ (try) to work as a stunt man, then as a roofer. Johnny (106)_____ (say) he (107)_____ (speak) to the police about helping Dangerfield when he (108)_____ (get) out of prison. In addition, if it's possible, Dangerfield (109)_____ (learn) a trade while he (110)_____ (be) in

prison. As he (111)_____ (learn) his new line of work, Johnny (112)_____
(counsel) him. By the time he (113)_____ (get) out of prison, he (114)_____
(become) a new man.

Well, Mom and Dad, I (115)_____ (go) on vacation soon. By the time this letter
(116)_____ (reach) you, I (117)_____ (live) on a farm in Nebraska for a
week. I (118)_____ (go) there with a guy named Elmer, Jr. Ever since I
(119)_____ (meet) him, he (120)_____ (tell) me about the wonderful life
in Nebraska. By the time we (121)_____ (leave) the city, I (122)_____
(hear) him say at least a hundred times how he (123)_____ (hate) life in the city. I
(124)_____ (look forward to) meeting his parents, who (125)_____
(celebrate) their 100th wedding anniversary next Saturday.

Your loving son.

RAP IT ALL UP

DIRECTIONS: Work in a group of 4 or more people. Pretend you are at Frankie's party. Look
at the pictures of the guests below, choose one person, and play the role of that person. Talk to the
other guests at the party. Ask each one to tell you about what he's done in the past, what he's doing
now, and what he plans to do. Learn as much as you can about each guest.

APPENDIX

IRREGULAR VERBS

Present	Past	Past Participle
arise	arose	arisen
be (am, is, are)	was, were	been
beat	beat	beaten
become	became	become
begin	began	begun
bend	bent	bent
bet	bet	bet
bid	bid	bid
bind	bound	bound
bite	bit	bitten
bleed	bled	bled
blow	blew	blown
break	broke	broken
breed	bred	bred
bring	brought	brought
build	built	built
burst	burst	burst
buy	bought	bought
cast	cast	cast
catch	caught	caught
choose	chose	chosen
cling	clung	clung
come	came	come
cost	cost	cost
creep	crept	crept
cut	cut	cut
deal	dealt	dealt
dig	dug	dug
do	did	done
draw	drew	drawn
dream	dreamed/dreamt	dreamed/dreamt
drink	drank	drunk
drive	drove	driven
eat	ate	eaten
fall	fell	fallen
feed	fed	fed
feel	felt	felt
fight	fought	fought
find	found	found
flee	fled	fled
fly	flew	flown
forbid	forbade/forbad	forbidden

Present	Past	Past Participle
forget	forgot	forgotten
forgive	forgave	forgiven
freeze	froze	frozen
get	got	gotten/got
give	gave	given
go	went	gone
grind	ground	ground
grow	grew	grown
hang	hung/hanged	hung/hanged
have	had	had
hear	heard	heard
hide	hid	hidden/hid
hit	hit	hit
hold	held	held
hurt	hurt	hurt
keep	kept	kept
kneel	knelt	knelt
know	knew	known
lay	laid	laid
lead	led	led
leave	left	left
lend	lent	lent
let	let	let
lie	lay	lain
light	lighted/lit	lighted/lit
lose	lost	lost
make	made	made
mean	meant	meant
meet	met	met
pay	paid	paid
put	put	put
quit	quit	quit
read	read	read
ride	rode	ridden
ring	rang	rung
rise	rose	risen
run	ran	run
say	said	said
see	saw	seen
seek	sought	sought
sell	sold	sold
send	sent	sent
set	set	set
shake	shook	shaken
shed	shed	shed
shine	shone/shined	shone/shined
shoot	shot	shot

Present	Past	Past Participle
shrink	shrank	shrunk
shut	shut	shut
sing	sang	sung
sink	sank	sunk
sit	sat	sat
slay	slew	slain
sleep	slept	slept
slide	slid	slid
slink	slunk	slunk
slit	slit	slit
speak	spoke	spoken
speed	sped	sped
spend	spent	spent
spin	spun	spun
spit	spit	spit
split	split	split
spread	spread	spread
spring	sprang	sprung
stand	stood	stood
steal	stole	stolen
stick	stuck	stuck
sting	stung	stung
stink	stank	stunk
string	strung	strung
strive	strove	striven
swear	swore	sworn
sweep	swept	swept
swim	swam	swum
swing	swung	swung
take	took	taken
teach	taught	taught
tear	tore	torn
tell	told	told
think	thought	thought
throw	threw	thrown
understand	understood	understood
wake	woke (vi), waked (vt.)	woken, waken
wear	wore	worn
weave	wove	woven
wed	wed	wed
weep	wept	wept
wet	wet	wet
win	won	won
wind	wound	wound
withdraw	withdrew	withdrawn
wring	wrung	wrung
write	wrote	written

NON-ACTION VERBS

The verbs in the column on the left are usually NON-ACTION VERBS; that is, they are *not usually used in any of the continuous tenses.* However, many of these verbs have two meanings; one NON-ACTION and the other ACTION.

VERBS	NON-ACTION	ACTION
CONDITION:		
be	He is tall.	He's being very good. (be = BEHAVE/ACT)
consist	It consists of eggs and milk.	
cost	This costs too much.	
equal	Two and four equal six.	
fit	The suit fits well.	The tailor is fitting him for a new suit. (fit = MEASURE FOR; CAUSE TO FIT OR CONFORM)
matter	It doesn't matter.	
owe	I owe him $10.00.	
resemble	She resembles her sister.	
weigh	He weighs 150 lbs.	He's weighing himself now. (weigh = PUT ON A SCALE)
POSSESSION:		
belong	That belongs to them.	
contain	This contains our dishes.	
have	I have a typewriter. (have = POSSESS)	I'm having some problems. (have = EXPERIENCE) He's having breakfast. (have = EAT/DRINK)
own	They own some property.	
possess	He possesses two houses.	

VERBS	NON-ACTION	ACTION
PERCEPTION:		
appear	He appears to be ready. (appear = SEEM)	She's appearing in a new play. (appear = PERFORM or COME INTO SIGHT)
feel	I feel it's a good idea. (feel = THINK/BELIEVE) He feels relieved. (feel = HAVE AN EMOTION)	I'm feeling better now. (feel = EXPERIENCE AN EMOTION OR PHYSICAL FEELING) She's feeling around for the light switch. (feel = TOUCH)
hear	He doesn't hear you. (hear = PERCEIVE WITH THE EARS)	You'll be hearing from my lawyer. (hear = GET A LETTER OR CALL) Judge Burr is hearing this case. (hear = JUDGE; LISTEN TO TESTIMONY)
look	You look tired. (look = SEEM)	He's looking at you. (look = USE ONE'S EYES)
see	I see him over there. (see = PERCEIVE WITH THE EYES)	The mayor is seeing her now. (see = MEET WITH)
seem	It seems like a good idea.	
smell	This smells good! (smell = HAVE A SMELL) I smell something odd. (smell = PERCEIVE A SMELL INVOLUNTARILY)	She's smelling every perfume in the store. (smell = SNIFF)
sound	That sounds good. (sound = SEEM)	They're sounding the alarm. (sound = CAUSE A SOUND)
taste	This tastes great! (taste = HAVE A TASTE) I taste something strange. (taste = PERCEIVE A TASTE INVOLUNTARILY)	He's tasting your cake now. (taste = TRY, SAMPLE FOOD)

VERBS	NON-ACTION	ACTION
EMOTIONAL/ MENTAL ACTIVITY:		
appreciate	I appreciate your suggestion.	
approve	He doesn't approve.	
believe	I believe her.	
desire	She desired to see them once again. (formal)	
dislike	I dislike being in crowds.	
doubt	He doubts that it's true.	
guess	I guess we should start. (guess = SUPPOSE)	He doesn't know for sure. He's just guessing. (guess = MAKE AN ESTIMATE)
hate	I hate this music.	
imagine	I imagine that you're tired. (imagine = GUESS, THINK)	You're just imagining things. (imagine = USE THE IMAGINATION)
know	She knows the president.	
like	We like to ski.	
love	They love their country.	
mean	It means "no." (mean = SIGNIFY)	I've been meaning to do that. (mean = INTEND)
mind	I don't mind. (mind = OBJECT TO)	Who's minding the store? (mind = TAKE CARE OF)
need*	We need a car.	
prefer	He prefers this one.	
recognize	I don't recognize anyone.	
remember	They don't remember anything.	
think	I think it's too big. (think = BELIEVE, HAVE AN OPINION)	Wait a second. I'm thinking. (think = CONSIDER, REFLECT)
understand	I understand what you're saying.	
want*	I don't want any right now.	

*NOTE: Although these verbs are not usually used with continuous tenses, they *are* frequently used with the PAST PERFECT CONTINUOUS and PRESENT PERFECT CONTINUOUS.

I*'ve been needing* a new coat for a long time.

He *had been wanting* that car for a long time when he finally bought it.

TENSES MOST COMMONLY USED IN SUBORDINATE CLAUSES

Although the following chart is not conclusive, it generally works for cases in this book and can be used as a reference. You will find that it is frequently impossible to use the tenses in Column 3 in *all types* of subordinate clauses. For example, if we take the first item on the chart, we find the following:

I'll help you after you had problems. (impossible)
I'll help you because you had a problem with that. (possible)
I'll help anyone who had a problem on the last exam. (possible)

The use of a certain tense in a subordinate clause is determined by the *type* of clause (adjective clause, adverb clause, clause of time, clause of reason, and so on) as well as by the type of verb.

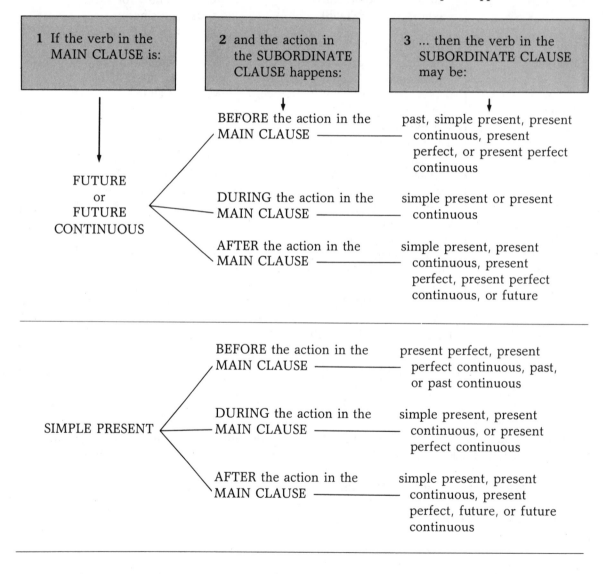

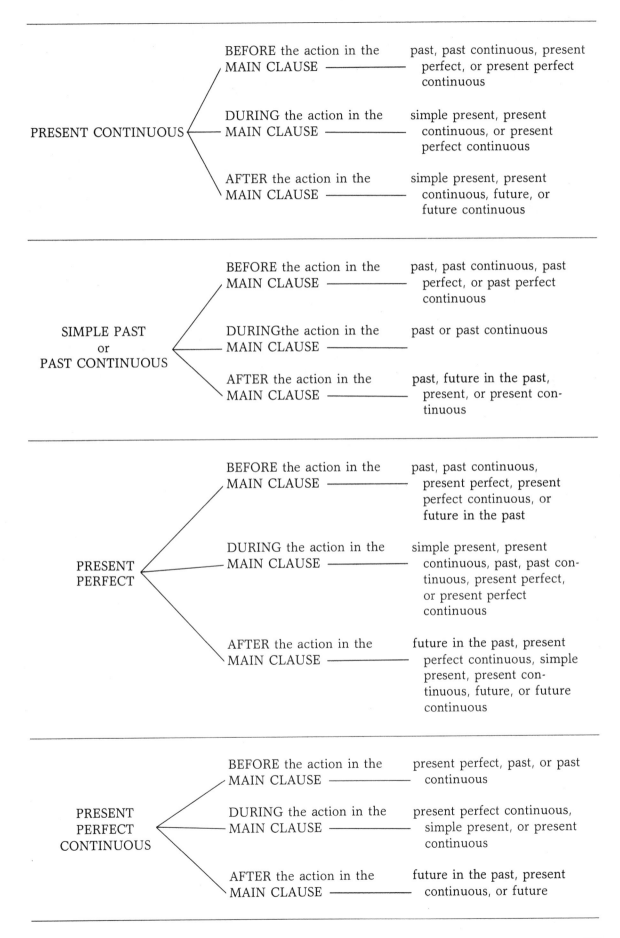

PRESENT CONTINUOUS

BEFORE the action in the MAIN CLAUSE —— past, past continuous, present perfect, or present perfect continuous

DURING the action in the MAIN CLAUSE —— simple present, present continuous, or present perfect continuous

AFTER the action in the MAIN CLAUSE —— simple present, present continuous, future, or future continuous

SIMPLE PAST or PAST CONTINUOUS

BEFORE the action in the MAIN CLAUSE —— past, past continuous, past perfect, or past perfect continuous

DURING the action in the MAIN CLAUSE —— past or past continuous

AFTER the action in the MAIN CLAUSE —— past, future in the past, present, or present continuous

PRESENT PERFECT

BEFORE the action in the MAIN CLAUSE —— past, past continuous, present perfect, present perfect continuous, or future in the past

DURING the action in the MAIN CLAUSE —— simple present, present continuous, past, past continuous, present perfect, or present perfect continuous

AFTER the action in the MAIN CLAUSE —— future in the past, present perfect continuous, simple present, present continuous, future, or future continuous

PRESENT PERFECT CONTINUOUS

BEFORE the action in the MAIN CLAUSE —— present perfect, past, or past continuous

DURING the action in the MAIN CLAUSE —— present perfect continuous, simple present, or present continuous

AFTER the action in the MAIN CLAUSE —— future in the past, present continuous, or future

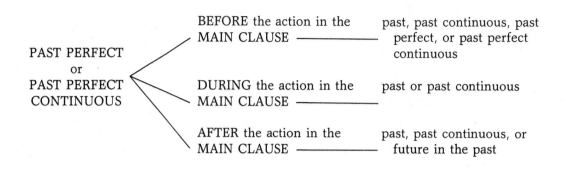

	BEFORE the action in the MAIN CLAUSE	past, past continuous, past perfect, or past perfect continuous
PAST PERFECT or PAST PERFECT CONTINUOUS	DURING the action in the MAIN CLAUSE	past or past continuous
	AFTER the action in the MAIN CLAUSE	past, past continuous, or future in the past

PASSIVE VOICE

	ACTIVE VOICE	**PASSIVE VOICE**
SIMPLE PRESENT	He *eats* lunch everyday.	Lunch *is eaten* everyday.
PRESENT CONTINUOUS	is eating	is being eaten
SIMPLE PAST	ate	was eaten
PAST CONTINUOUS	was eating	was being eaten
PRESENT PERFECT	has eaten	has been eaten
PAST PERFECT	had eaten	had been eaten
SIMPLE FUTURE	will eat	will be eaten
FUTURE PERFECT	will have eaten	will have been eaten

NOTE: In the passive sentence we use the word "by" with the subject of the active sentence only if it offers important information.

Example: ACTIVE: The mayor wrote the letter.
PASSIVE: The letter was written by the mayor.

INDIRECT SPEECH

	DIRECT SPEECH	INDIRECT SPEECH
SIMPLE PRESENT	"I eat"	I said (that) I ate
PRESENT CONTINUOUS	"I am eating"	I said (that) I was eating
SIMPLE PAST	"I ate"	I said (that) I had eaten
PAST CONTINUOUS	"I was eating"	I said (that) I had been eating
PRESENT PERFECT	"I have eaten"	I said (that) I had eaten
PRESENT PERFECT CONTINUOUS	"I have been eating"	I said (that) I had been eating
PAST PERFECT	"I had eaten"	I said (that) I had eaten
PAST PERFECT CONTINUOUS	"I had been eating"	I said (that) I had been eating
SIMPLE FUTURE	"I will eat" "I am going to eat"	I said (that) I would eat I said (that) I was going to eat
FUTURE CONTINUOUS	"I will be eating"	I said (that) I would be eating
FUTURE PERFECT	"I will have eaten"	I said (that) I would have eaten
FUTURE PERFECT CONTINUOUS	"I will have been eating"	I said (that) I would have been eating

REAL/POSSIBLE

FUTURE	if + present/present continuous	be going to + simple form will + simple form present continuous

If I remember, I'll call him tomorrow.

PRESENT	if + present	present

If I remember, I usually call him once a week.

PAST	if + past	past

If he saw you, why didn't he say hello?
(It's possible that he actually saw you.)

UNREAL

FUTURE or PRESENT	past/* if + past continuous	would/could + simple form

If I had a good memory, I would remember to call.
  (REAL SITUATION: I don't have a good memory, so I don't remember
  to call.)

PAST	if + past perfect (continuous)	would have + past participle could have + past participle

If I had remembered, I would have called him.
  (REAL SITUATION: I didn't remember, so I didn't call him.)

NOTE: The verb "be" in this case is always "were."

If I were you, I would call more often.

ON	⛶		CITY	🏙
IN	⊠		DAY	☼
UNDER	⍞		HOME/HOUSE	🏠
OVER	⍞		NEGATIVE	(VERB)
NEXT TO	☐×		NIGHT	☾
BY	⊟→		SUNRISE	☼↑
AROUND	(☐↻)		SUNSET	☼↓
OFF	⬜↱		MORNING	A.M.
OUT	⬜↱		EVENING	P.M.
AT	@		EXPENSIVE	$↑
UP	↑			
TO	→			
DOWN	↓			
WITH	w/			
WITHOUT	w/out			

CHAPTER 1 (PRESENT CONTINUOUS/SIMPLE PRESENT)

1. own
2. sail
3. take
4. sells
5. are arriving
6. are carrying
7. are renting
8. is
9. stands
10. signals
11. is daydreaming
12. is loosening
13. throwing
14. starts
15. prepares
    is preparing
16. gives
17. finds
18. drops
19. throw
20. are fishing
21. is telling
22. are eating
23. don't feel
    aren't feeling
24. are trying
25. is reeling
26. is taking
27. are helping
28. is also trying
29. always tries
    is always trying
30. ends up
31. is forever tripping
32. falling
33. getting
34. are helping
    (help)
35. is leaning
36. is jumping
37. seems
38. is winning
39. is falling
40. knows

CHAPTER 2 (PRESENT PERFECT/SIMPLE PRESENT)

Elmer's brother, Norbert, is 97 and lives alone in the city. He's lived there since he left the farm 75 years ago. He's had an apartment on the top floor of a tall building (high-rise) for the past 20 years.

Norbert is a very charming person, so he has a lot of friends, and he leads a busy life. He almost never gets out of bed before noon (twelve) each morning because he usually stays up late at night. He likes to play cards with his friends in the afternoon. Sometimes he goes to the horse races, and he always wins a lot of money. In the evening he usually takes his girlfriend to an expensive restaurant. He's known her for over 30 years, but he doesn't feel that he's ready to get married.

Norbert knows that many people spend every afternoon in the park, where they sit on a bench and feed the birds. But he's never gone into the park since he came to the city because he thinks that only elderly people go to parks.

Every summer, he takes a train down to his brother's farm and spends some time there. He's there right now. He's only been there for five days, but he's ready to go back to the city.

Norbert and his brother Elmer are very different from each other, and they've argued about everything ever since Norbert arrived on Tuesday. The problem is that Norbert's never liked the life of a farmer. He's complained for four days about getting up at dawn (sunrise) and helping Elmer with the cows. He's fed the chickens and gathered eggs all week, but he hasn't enjoyed it. The truth is that Norbert hates animals. He thinks that horses belong in the races and birds belong in the park, and he's sure that people belong in a city!

Elmer's wife, Iona, has been worried about Norbert's health for many years. She's fed him homemade soup and fresh vegetables all week, and she's made (makes) him go to bed at 9:00 every night. Norbert's worst problem is that she's tried since Tuesday to persuade him to settle down and get married to his girlfriend. He's heard this from her for many years. Every time, he sighs and tells her the same thing: that he's been a bachelor all his life, and he doesn't want to change now.

CHAPTER 3 (PRESENT PERFECT CONTINUOUS/PRESENT CONTINUOUS)

1. has been doing
2. is working
   has been working
3. is always volunteering
   (see page 6, #3)
4. is constantly sweeping
5. cleaning
6. has been doing
7. has been working
8. has been peeling
9. chopping
10. washing
11. is Joey doing
    has Joey been doing
12. is working
13. has been trying
14. are bringing
    have been bringing
15. is using
    has been using
16. is staying up
    has been staying up
17. are only waiting
    have only been waiting
18. is looking
19. is talking
20. is pulling
21. is trying
    has been trying
22. has been trying
23. is always looking
24. has been bribing
25. stealing
26. sawing

SUPPLEMENTARY EXERCISE

1. have been doing
   (have done)
2. have often seen
3. has been
4. has been mopping
   (has mopped)
5. has been studying
   (has studied)
6. have known
7. has owed
8. has never been
9. has written
10. has seemed

CHAPTER 4 (PRESENT TENSE REVIEW)

1. are trying
2. are wiggling
3. screaming
4. chasing
5. is going
   has been going
6. has been waiting on
   has waited on
7. don't fit (see page 155)
8. thinks
9. has been having
   has had
   is having
10. has been running
    has run
11. a, has been trying on*
    b, has tried on
12. a, not putting
    b, not put
13. has been walking
    has walked
14. have been killing
    (This idiom is always used
    with continuous tenses.)
15. walks
16. tries
17. is doing
    does
18. hasn't caught
19. refuses
20. is standing
21. looks
22. sees
23. is walking
24. doesn't see
25. isn't wearing
26. is beginning
27. is tearing
28. (has been regretting)
    has regretted
29. is

*NOTE: If you've chosen answer a, then the following answer must also be a, and so on.

CHAPTER 5 (SIMPLE PAST/PRESENT PERFECT)

Oscar's wife, Regina, has driven him crazy for years. On their wedding day, they swore to stick together forever, but the romance died soon after the honeymoon.

Oscar has always been rich, but he's never been interested in his money. He's always wanted a simple life. Before he got married, he liked to go camping. He often went hiking up in the mountains. He sat next to a stream in the shade of a big tree or lay in a hammock for hours. On weekends, he liked to stay home and mow the lawn.

However, Oscar's life has been very different since his marriage. Oscar and Regina have gone on four cruises around the world in the past five years. Regina has insisted on Oscar buying her so much jewelry that last April he gave up and bought a diamond mine. Regina withdrew one third of the money in their bank account last year, and she has withdrawn another third this year.

Recently, the situation has gotten even worse. Last month, Regina tore up the lawn in the back yard and tore down Oscar's hammock. After that, she threw out his favorite fishing pole, hiking boots, and tent.

Oscar has had an ulcer for years. His doctor has often told him to take it easy and to stop smoking and drinking. But Oscar and Regina have just recently found a solution to both Oscar's ulcer and their marriage problems. Last week, Regina agreed to go fishing with Oscar up in the mountains. In return, Oscar agreed to buy Regina a mink tent. They went on their fishing trip and had a great time. They haven't argued about anything since then.

CHAPTER 6 (PAST CONTINUOUS/SIMPLE PAST)

1. happened
2. were having
3. happened
4. was digging
5. was punching
6. was checking
7. matched
   (was matching)
8. was ordering
9. was repairing
10. were doing
11. began
12. was oiling
13. sounded
14. began
15. stopped
16. were doing
17. were trying
18. was ringing
19. appeared
20. seemed
21. landed
22. held
    (were holding)
23. watched
    (were watching)
24. opened
25. stepped
26. hid
27. began
28. began
29. approached
    (were approaching)
30. reached
31. ran
32. began
33. climbed
    (was climbing)
34. saw
35. looked

CHAPTER 7 (FUTURE IN THE PAST/SIMPLE PAST)

Frankie woke up one day last year and decided that it was going to be (would be) a good day for him. He picked up his guitar and went to his usual place in the park. He put down his guitar case and began to play. He was sure a lot of people were going to come (would come) to listen to him play.

At first, the park was very quiet. There were only a few squirrels and birds who came by because they thought Frankie was going to give (would give) them something to eat. Then a lot of people began to rush by Frankie on their way to work, but he knew they weren't going to put (wouldn't put) any money in his guitar case because they were in a hurry.

Frankie played all morning and thought about his future. He knew that he wasn't going to become (wouldn't become) a famous rock star (singer, musician) in the future. He realized that he was never going to have (would never have) a big house with a swimming pool. He knew that he was never going to be able (would never be able) to buy an expensive car. He was sure that he was never going to travel (would never travel) around the world on a ship. He began to feel really sad.

At about noon, a policewoman came by. For a minute, Frankie was afraid that she was going to arrest (would arrest) him (or at least chase him out of the park) for playing without a permit. But the policewoman just stopped, sat down on a bench, and listened to him. After a few minutes, the policewoman got up, put some money in Frankie's guitar case, and said, "You play very well!"

Then the policewoman told Frankie that she had a brother who worked for a radio station in another city. She said she would talk (was going to talk) with him on the telephone later that day and that she would ask (was going to ask) her brother to have Frankie play his guitar on his radio program.

Well, of course Frankie was thrilled. He began to dream that maybe he really would become (was going to become) a famous rock star (singer, musician). Maybe he would be able (was going to be able) to buy a big house and an expensive car. Maybe he would travel (was going to travel) around the world on a ship. Maybe ....

CHAPTER 8 (RECAP)

1. has lived
2. have tried
3. has been
4. decided
5. would build
   were going to build
6. sent
7. were going to buy
   would buy
8. would have to
   was going to have to
9. told
10. wouldn't move
    wasn't going to move
11. began
12. sent
13. got
14. found
15. was sitting
16. were wondering
17. appeared
18. chased
19. were screaming
20. running
21. arrived
22. took
23. started
24. was hiding
    hid
25. made
    was making
26. clung
    was clinging
27. growled
    was growling
28. sat
29. asked
30. was happening
31. appeared
32. became
33. were
34. decided
35. wouldn't build
    weren't going to build
36. was
37. threw
38. has been
39. have noticed
40. has become

CHAPTER 9 (PAST PERFECT/SIMPLE PAST)

1. went
2. had never been
3. were
4. had gone
5. had been
6. looked (see p. 160)
7. had slept
8. had looked
9. were
10. had been
11. ate
12. slept
13. fought
14. played
15. had done
16. drove
17. stuck
18. gave
19. told
20. was
21. were
22. came
23. drove
24. had never seen
25. didn't get
   (= have an opportunity)
26. had dived
27. was
28. had forgotten
29. was
30. had fed
31. had been (at Lion Country Safari)
   was (in general)

CHAPTER 10 (PAST PERFECT CONTINUOUS/PAST CONTINUOUS/SIMPLE PAST)

Dudley Dangerfield had been looking forward to his vacation for a long time when he finally got to Hawaii. He had been working very hard and needed to relax. On his first day at the hotel, he laid his towel on the beach and lay down on it. He put on his sunglasses and began to read a book on flying. He had been thinking about practicing his flying ever since he had almost fallen out of the plane several years earlier. While he was reading, he fell asleep. When he woke up, he realized that he had been sleeping for three hours, and his first day was almost over.

On his second day, he was lying in a hammock under a palm tree when he started to think about his health. He was a little overweight because he had been eating a lot of terrific international food ever since he had gotten his first job as a spy. He decided to go on a diet, sweat in the sauna every day, and jog five miles every morning. He was thinking (had been thinking) about getting in shape for the Annual International Spy Tennis Tournament when suddenly he heard a loud scream from somewhere down the beach.

He jumped up and ran down the beach to see what the commotion was. He saw a woman in the water. She was screaming and thrashing around and appeared to be drowning. On the beach, a few people were running around and trying to find a lifeguard. Dudley jumped in, swam out, and pulled her to shore. Someone on the beach spread a towel on the sand, and Dudley put her on it. Someone else in the crowd said that the woman had been trying to swim to shore from a yacht. Finally, the woman opened her eyes, and Dudley saw that she was fine. He also noticed that she was gorgeous. He was quickly falling in love with her when the police ran up and arrested her. They said that she was an international criminal who had been following Dudley for several weeks. She had been planning to kidnap him for her government since the first of the month. The police had been trying to capture her since she had gotten to Hawaii.

That evening, while the sun was slowly setting, Dudley took a walk up the beach. As he was walking (walked), he thought with regret about his would-be romance. He considered exploring a new line of work.

CHAPTER 11 (PAST TENSE REVIEW)

1. began
2. was
3. hadn't ever gone
   had never gone
4. hadn't been eating
   hadn't eaten
5. joined
6. was
7. had been worrying
   had worried
8. ran
9. swam
10. took
11. sweated
12. thought
13. was sweating
    sweated
14. dreamed/dreamt
    was dreaming
15. had told
    ("at that time" =
    before that time)
16. was changing
17. thinking
18. came
19. told
20. had just begun
21. was
22. said
23. told
24. had mentioned
25. went
26. walked
27. was giving
28. was pointing
    pointed
29. had put
30. sank
31. saw
32. said
33. had been coming
34. teaching
    had taught
35. told
36. had weighed
37. started
38. was
39. swore
40. was
41. was eating
    ate
42. thought
    was thinking
43. had changed
    was changing
44. had become
    was becoming
45. hadn't eaten
46. had been exercising
    had exercised
47. had been thinking
    had thought
48. had tried
49. was drinking
    drank
50. remembered
51. had recently left
52. had become
    was becoming
53. had preferred
    preferred
54. had traded in

CHAPTER 12 (CUMULATIVE REVIEW)

I.
1. was
2. got
3. stuck
4. set
5. sold
6. learned
7. have loved
8. worked
   was working
9. wasn't
10. were forever going
    (see page 51, #6)
11. began
12. had already shut
13. was sitting
14. had already eaten
15. were growing
    had grown
16. thought
17. was going to throw
    would throw
18. were
19. began
20. led
21. looked
22. traveled
23. had been seeing
    ("see" = find)
    had seen
24. had been warning
    had warned
25. had been threatening
    had threatened
    was threatening
26. gave
27. watched
28. went
    was going
29. were doing
30. was getting
31. had been
32. was doing
33. were trying
34. yelled
    was yelling
35. had already climbed
36. had just stepped
    were just stepping

II.
37. happened
38. had caught
39. sneezed
40. lost
41. crashed
42. looked
43. lost
44. caught
45. fell
    was falling
46. hung
47. was sweating
48. saw
49. had collapsed
50. had fallen
51. held
    was holding
52. clung
53. let
54. was
55. was going to faint
    would faint
56. knew

57. would probably break
    was probably going to break
58. fell
59. slid
60. landed
61. was
62. fled
63. had just squeezed
64. were now trying
65. ran
66. split
67. was trying
68. headed
69. was running
70. was wondering
71. would happen
    was going to happen
72. sprang

73. fled
74. hid
75. was
76. chose
77. was forever happening
    (see page 51, #6)

III. 78. began
79. ended
80. waited on
81. went
82. have worked
    have been working
83. graduated
84. is
    has been
85. sit
86. have
87. answer

88. give
89. comes
90. asks
91. stole
92. have tried
93. happens
94. am sitting
95. hoping
96. am daydreaming
97. am beginning
    have begun
98. have worn
99. have answered
100. haven't done
101. isn't
102. have seen
     have been seeing
103. have already decided

CHAPTER 13 (SIMPLE FUTURE: WILL/BE GOING TO)

1. will be
   is going to be ⎫
2. will be   ⎬ prediction
   is going to be ⎭
3. will fire (promise)
   is going to fire (plan)
4. hire
5. will fix (promise)
   are going to fix (plan or prediction)
6. will serve (promise)
   are going to serve (plan)
7. will have (promise)
8. will cut
9. will have (promise)
   is going to have (plan)
10. will work (prediction)
    is going to work (plan or prediction)
11. will give (prediction)
    is going to give (plan or prediction)
12. is going to promise (plan)

13. will make (promise)
    is going to make (plan)
14. is going to provide (Lionel's plan)
15. is going to stop
16. is going to buy ⎫
17. is going to work ⎬ plan
18. is going to draw ⎭
19. glue
20. will say (prediction)
    are going to say (plan)
21. will cut out (promise or determination)
22. will be able (promise)
    are going to be able (plan)
23. will have to (promise or determination)
    are going to have to (plan)
24. will find (determination)
25. will be
    is going to be
26. is going to give (plan)
27. will be

CHAPTER 14 (SIMPLE PRESENT/SIMPLE FUTURE: WILL/BE GOING TO)

Esmeralda sees that she'll have (she's going to have) problems with money in the future if she doesn't change her way of doing business. She'll have (is going to have) three main problems.

First, people will begin (are going to begin) to drive by her little shop on their way to big shopping centers. They won't see (aren't going to see) her sign in the window in their hurry to get to a big store.

Another problem will be (is going to be) her eyesight. As she gets older, her eyesight will get (is going to get) worse. In the future, it'll be (it's going to be) difficult for her to see images in her crystal ball.

But Esmeralda's worst problem will be (is going to be) that people will stop (are going to stop) believing in gypsies with crystal balls because they'll think (they're going to think) that crystal balls are out of style. When they do that, they'll stop going (they're going to stop going) to fortune tellers, and Esmeralda's business will be (is going to be) in terrible trouble. Young people won't beg (aren't going to beg) her for advice on romance anymore. Rock stars won't offer (aren't going to offer) her money and jewelry for advice on music. Detectives won't ask (aren't going to ask) her for help in catching criminals.

As soon as Esmeralda makes some big changes in her business, she'll stop (she's going to stop) worrying, and she won't have any more trouble with ulcers. But because she'll always be (is always going to be) a stubborn, independent woman, she'll refuse (she's going to refuse) to make any changes until the city government decides to evict her and tear down her house (shop). When they do that, she'll have to (she's going to have to) move her business to a shopping center. After she moves, she'll get (she's going to get) some glasses and buy advertising in all the local newspapers. Then she'll throw (she's going to throw) out her crystal ball and buy a computer.

As soon as a customer sees her computer, he'll know (he's going to know) that Esmeralda is a very modern fortune teller. Soon, thousands of people will begin (are going to begin) to come to her new shop. She'll hire (is going to hire) more people and open branch offices. Every office will have (is going to have) a computer. In a few years, she'll have (she's going to have) a whole chain of offices, and business will be (is going to be) terrific!

CHAPTER 15 (PRESENT CONTINUOUS/SIMPLE FUTURE: WILL/BE GOING TO)

1. will really like
    are really going to like
2. will be
    is going to be
3. will do
    are going to do
    are doing
4. will have to
    are going to have to
5. are loading
6. will count
    (volunteered action)
7. are loading
8. will watch
    (volunteered action)
9. will get
    are going to get
10. are doing
11. will get
    (volunteered action)
12. will finish
    are going to finish
13. will read
14. are driving
15. will unload
    are going to unload
16. will ring
17. will hold
18. are carrying
19. are spreading
20. will listen
21. will watch
22. are rolling (see page 158)
23. will tell (promise)
24. will be
25. are finishing
26. will go
27. will hand
28. are hammering
29. will clean up
    are going to clean up
30. will tell
31. will be
    is going to be
32. are you going to go
    are you going (plan)
33. will be
    am going to be (prediction)
34. won't get
    aren't going to get

CHAPTER 16 (FUTURE CONTINUOUS/SIMPLE FUTURE: WILL/BE GOING TO/PRESENT CONTINUOUS (meaning the future))

My parents are bringing (are going to bring/will be bringing) my new baby brother home from the hospital tomorrow morning, and life will be (is going to be) just terrible for me. My parents won't pay (aren't going to pay) any attention to me anymore. While my mother is feeding him, I'll be doing my homework without any help. While I'm reading my school books out loud, my father won't be listening because he'll be playing with my baby brother. While I'm swinging in the backyard, my brother will be crawling across the lawn, so my parents won't be watching me. As my brother is growing up, I'll be shrinking into the background.

However, I have a plan. At midnight (twelve) tomorrow night, I'll be hiding (I'll hide/I'm going to hide) under my brother's crib, and I'll wait (I'm going to wait) until my parents are sleeping. Then I'll grab (I'm going to grab/I'm grabbing) my brother and quietly creep (creeping*) out of the house. I'll get (I'm going to get/I'm getting) on a bus and take (taking*) him back to the hospital. I'll trade (I'm going to trade/I'm trading) him in on something else: maybe a dog or a horse or a robot.

On the other hand, maybe I won't steal him. If I do, the police will probably arrest (are probably going to arrest) me for kidnapping. My mother will probably faint (is probably going to faint), and my father will yell (is going to yell) a lot and tear out his hair. No, I won't trade him in. Instead, I'll teach (I'm going to teach) him things. For example, I'll teach him to play Hide and Seek. While I'm hiding, he'll be looking for me. And I'll teach him to ride a bicycle (bike) and build a toy house and float in the pool. I'll teach him about the animals in the zoo, too. Of course, while he's learning all these things, my parents will be ignoring me. I'll be teaching him all day long, but my parents will probably think (are probably going to think) he's a genius.

I know what I'll do (I'm going to do). I'll run (I'm going to run) away from home! One night, when my parents are sleeping, I'll pack (I'm going to pack/I'm packing) my suitcase (bag) and quietly creep (creeping*) out of the house. I'll get (I'm going to get/I'm getting) on a bus and leave (leaving*) the city far behind. While my little brother is growing up, he'll wish (he's going to wish/he'll be wishing) he had a big sister to teach him about bicycles (bikes) and pools and animals and parents!

*NOTE: With compound verbs, the two actions should be in the same form, but the auxilliary verbs are omitted from the second action.

CHAPTER 17 (FUTURE PERFECT/SIMPLE FUTURE: WILL/BE GOING TO/ SIMPLE PRESENT)

1. will have run
2. will have stuck
3. will have fallen
4. rings
5. will have lost
6. will have torn
7. will finally come
   is finally going to come
8. will be
   is going to be
9. will have heard
10. won't have understood
11. will have explained
12. arrives

13. will get
    is going to get
14. will take
    is going to take
15. recover
16. will have failed
17. fail
18. will promise
    are going to promise
19. rolls around
20. will be
    is going to be
21. will have complained
22. will have gotten

23. will be
    is going to be
24. will sit
    is going to sit
25. sweat
26. return
27. will have forgotten
28. will take
    is going to take
29. will have considered
30. will have sworn
31. begins
32. will be
    is going to be

CHAPTER 18 (FUTURE PERFECT CONTINUOUS/FUTURE CONTINUOUS/ SIMPLE PRESENT (meaning the future))

Dear Rebecca,

When you come up out of your diving bell in a few weeks, your father and I'll be waiting for you on the ship. By that time, we will have been looking forward to your visit for four years - ever since you chose this strange line of work and went down there.

While we wait aboard the ship, your brothers and sisters will be decorating the house and fixing an enormous meal (without any fish at all). As we drive home, they'll be preparing your favorite foods, and your nieces and nephews will be chasing each other around, sticking their hands into the cake, and pulling the dog's tail. When we arrive home, they all will be standing on the front porch. After everyone hugs and kisses, we'll be catching up on the news all weekend.

When you and Leonard get to the surface, you'll be having meetings with famous scientists from all over the world, and newspaper reporters will be interviewing you because you will have been doing important experiments and discovering new species of fish. Unfortunately, I won't have been doing anything very interesting. I will just have been washing dishes, balancing the budget, tearing out coupons from the newspaper, and trying to figure out how to persuade you to come up out of your diving bell and stay with us on dry land!

> Love,
> Mom

CHAPTER 19 (FUTURE TENSE REVIEW)

1. is going to lead
   is leading
2. will be
   is going to be
3. is going to retire
   will be retiring
   is retiring
4. will have explored
5. will also have seen
6. is especially looking
7. will take
   is going to take
   is taking
8. will be
9. are working
10. are staying
11. are studying
12. preparing
13. will be taking
    will take
    are going to take
14. turn out
15. will be
    are going to be
16. is going to leave
    is leaving
    leaves
17. will check
    is going to check
    will be checking
18. don't pass
    (see page 158)
19. will be
    is going to be
    is
20. is visiting
    visits
21. will be photographing
    will photograph
    are going to photograph
22. are filming
    film
23. will be
    is going to be
24. will think
    are going to think
25. is (see page 158)
26. will catch
    is going to catch
27. watch
    are watching
28. will scream
    is going to scream
29. will run
    is going to run
30. will be filming
31. runs
32. is thanking
33. will spin
    is going to spin
34. bite
35. will promise
    is going to promise
36. will never rescue
37. is going to visit
    is visiting
38. finds
39. will be flirting
40. will get
    is going to get
41. start
42. will punch
    is going to punch
43. will have just recovered
44. will promise
    is going to promise
45. will never fall
46. arrive
47. will be conducting
    will conduct
    is going to conduct
48. is going to study
    will be studying

49. finds (see page 158)
50. is doing
51. will kidnap
    is going to kidnap
52. take
53. will try
    is going to try
54. won't let
    aren't going to let

55. is trying
    tries
56. will be watching
57. will bring
    are going to bring
58. will have attempted
59. meets
60. will fall
    is going to fall

61. won't return
    isn't going to return
62. will live
    is going to live
63. do I know
64. will happen
    is going to happen
65. is

CHAPTER 20 (CUMULATIVE REVIEW)

I. 1. am meeting
      have met
      have been meeting
   2. began
   3. met
   4. had just returned
   5. told
   6. started
      had started
   7. made
      had made
   8. was
      had been
   9. thought
      had thought
  10. were both
      both were
      had both been
  11. became
      had become
  12. became
  13. asked
  14. provided
  15. needed
  16. were climbing
  17. had
  18. fell
  19. fell
  20. finally managed
  21. told
  22. reached
      had reached
  23. found (see page 160)
  24. have met
  25. left
  26. attended
  27. didn't know
      hadn't known
  28. wanted

29. thought
30. would be
    was going to be
31. dreamed
32. would follow
    were going to follow
33. beg
34. thought
35. would spend
    was going to spend
36. spends
37. are
38. forgets
39. is trying
40. is attending
41. taking
42. is planning
    plans
43. finishes
44. will move
    is going to move
    is moving
45. don't know (see page 158)
46. lead

II. 47. was
    48. is (in general)
        was (at the party)
    49. was
    50. hasn't always been
        hadn't always been
        wasn't always
    51. said
    52. became
    53. inspired
    54. has been doing
        had done
    55. met
    56. will have followed
        will have been following

57. isn't wasting
    doesn't waste
58. gets up
59. runs
60. swims
61. has been
62. found out
63. had seen
    had been seeing
64. recognized
65. walked
66. shook
67. began
68. wins
69. will provide
    is going to provide
70. said
71. would balance (promise)
72. improve
73. applauded
74. promised
75. won't let
76. won't rest
77. will promote

III. 78. was finishing
         had finished
     79. burst
     80. rushed
     81. grabbed
     82. was flirting
         had been flirting
     83. began
     84. had been talking
         was talking
     85. stopped
     86. saw
     87. fainted
     88. arrested
     89. were taking

90. told
91. had been working
92. hadn't already fired
93. had had
94. had filled
    had been filling
95. had been starving
96. decided
97. had caught
98. discovered
99. was really feeling
100. told
101. introduced
102. had decided
103. knew
104. had worked
    had been working
105. had tried
106. said
107. would speak (promise/volunteered
    action)
    was going to speak (plan)
108. got (indirect speech)
109. will learn
    is going to learn
110. is

111. learns
    is learning
112. will be counseling
    will counsel
    is going to be counseling
113. gets
114. will have become
115. am going to go
    am going
116. reaches
117. will have been living
    will have lived
118. am going
    am going to go
119. met
120. has told
    has been telling
121. leave
122. will have heard
123. hates
124. am looking forward to
125. are celebrating
    will be celebrating
    will celebrate
    are going to celebrate